Advance

MW00777950

"*Aspire to Better: The 21st Century Electric Cooperative* gives a detailed account of major developments within the electric cooperative program and how they were shaped by individuals as well as outside forces. Mark Glaess observed much of this history firsthand and knows where many of the bodies are buried. Mark also has an excellent understanding of the values that enabled electric cooperative members to provide for themselves what no utility would offer to them. This book also gives examples where leaders have strayed from those values and the cost to the members greatly. A very impressive effort that should be required reading for all electric cooperative managers and directors."

—GLENN ENGLISH, retired CEO/National Rural Electric Cooperative Association, and former Oklahoma Member of Congress

"*Aspire to better* is a thought provoking read. Over 23 chapters, the book offers up some praise for the past accomplishments of rural electrification. But quickly, it challenges electric cooperatives and their leaders to an array of thought-provoking subjects, ranging from board governance to climate change response. This is a book for those who don't believe the future is assured by resting on their laurels."

—Dennis Hill, retired CEO, North Dakota Association of Rural Electric Cooperatives

"With congenial humor, relevant biblical passages, meticulous research, and wisdom born of deep experience, *Aspire to Better* is a treasure trove of common sense, bold new ideas, and lots of little nudges to our better angels for returning electric cooperatives to their original mission of "improving the lives of their members.

"Mark Glaess, in *Aspire to Better* integrates the best of what cooperative utilities have done, but does not shy away from taking them to task for their failures and deficiencies. The result is a veritable strategic, yet imminently implementable, plan for how co-ops can return to their original mission: Improving the lives of their members.

"There's a lot of wisdom and 'tough love' packed into these pages. Glaess has issued a clarion call to the current generation of electricity cooperative leaders, backed by a practical roadmap for staying focused on their original mission of 'improving the lives of their members.'"

—JASON MAKANSI, consultant and author of *Lights Out! The Electricity Crisis, the Global Economy, and What It Means To You* (2007), *Carbon IRA + YouTility: How to Address Climate Change & Reward Carbon Reduction Before It's Too Late* (2018), and *Painting By Numbers: How to Sharpen Your BS Detector and Smoke Out the "Experts"* (2016)

"If you want your co-op to be the utility of choice, then you need to buy this book. I've already ordered copies for my board and key staff."

—TIM THOMPSON, CEO, Lake Region Electric (Minnesota)

"During my career in the rural electric industry, I had the good fortune to work with incredible leaders, mentors, and innovators, but Mark Glaess is in a class of his own. As one of the most knowledgeable, forward thinking, and connected executives in the industry, Mark has a reputation of asking the hard questions and challenging the norms of the industry, in a quest to continually evolve and improve the value the industry delivers to its' 43 million Member / Owners.

"*Aspire to better: The 21st Century Electric Cooperative* is an important chronology of the industry. If we do not honor the past of the rural electric industry, celebrate our successes, and learn from our failures, we will not be effective in meeting the rapidly changing needs and future expectation of our Members.

"The next ten years will present the most significant challenges and opportunities our industry has experienced in its history. As we transition from the central station / carbon-based tenets of our industry, Mark challenges us to embrace innovation and the inevitable changes with courage and a sense of responsibility and service to our Members.

"Mark's book is an honest, if not at times uncomfortable, historical commentary and assessment of an industry and movement which is arguably one of the most successful and impactful government / private partnerships in the history of our nation. *Aspire to better: The 21st Century Electric Cooperative* is a reflection on our past and a roadmap for the future."

—Vern Dosch, CEO / President (retired) National
Information Solutions Cooperative (NISC)

"There are few people that know electric cooperatives and the electric cooperative business model as well as Mark. He has seen and heard it all - and can recall in vivid detail so much of the electric cooperative history and legacy. Mark was one of the first to recognize the challenges, changes, and opportunities coming to electric cooperatives, such as technology advancements, increased customer expectations, distributed generation, and so much more.

"In his new book, *Aspire to be Better: The 21st Century Electric Cooperative*, Mark uses his vast knowledge and understanding of electric cooperatives to provide helpful insight and direction for current and future electric cooperative leaders, as well as those simply interested in the electric cooperative business model and how it needs to prepare itself differently for the 21st century."

—Gary Connett, Co-Chair, Beneficial Electrification League

"You could skip to the 23rd chapter which lists 25 ideas toward the "Making of the Twenty-First Century Electric Cooperative," to gain an appreciation for Mark Glaess' seminal book entitled: *Aspire to Better: The 21st Century Electric Cooperative.* Doing so, however, skips the astonishing history of electric cooperatives, much which would have been lost had it not been for Glaess' research. Above all, this book, is a primer each co-op board member and staff must read to answer the question first posed when rural electrification was first voiced, and then voiced again in 2013: "Can we do it again?"

—Steve Collier, experienced public power professional,
executive, consultant, presenter, writer.

"Over Mark Glaess' 35 plus years of leadership and advocacy for rural electric cooperatives spanning a geography from Oregon to Minnesota, he has been a visionary never willing to accept the status quo or scared to challenge conventional wisdom. His hard work and insight on legislative and regulatory issues has stood the test of time for the electric cooperative model and cemented a legacy for the industry dating back to the 1930s. His book is a must read for electric cooperative leadership in the 21st century."

—BILL COLLET, Collet & Associates

"Mark is a talented thinker and writer. Readers may find much to disagree with, but *Aspire to Better: The 21st Century Electric Cooperative* will encourage important conversations regarding the future of this great electric cooperative program."

—MIKE WILLIAMS, Chair NRECA 21st Century Committee and CEO of the Texas Electric Cooperatives

"*Aspire* is a compelling narrative, well researched and thought provoking. Based on solid research and the author's distinguished career, *Aspire* skillfully frames essential policy issues which will affect the future of rural electrification. This book is thought provoking and important read for directors and managers. To that, *Aspire to Better: The 21st Century Electric Cooperative*, defines a strategic look at the difficult issues faced by rural electric leaders and provides a clarion call for the future. *Aspire* is a must read for directors and managers."

—JEFF NELSON, retired General Manager, East River Electric Power Cooperative

"Mark Glaess writes with wit and passion; he clearly knows cooperatives. *Aspire to Better* describes the cooperative landscape today, laying out the threats as well the incredible opportunities available to cooperatives who are visionary, and member focused. This book is a must read for every cooperative director wanting to keep their cooperative vital and relevant in the 21st Century and beyond."

—LINDA LAITALA, Board Chair, East Central Energy, Braham, Minnesota

"If you work for the electric cooperative industry, you must read this book. It's the quintessential Mark Glaess. The blender of rock and roll lyrics and biblical passages into his speeches as Statewide Manager of Minnesota. The sage, the visionary, the awesome predictor, the doer. I promise, you will be impressed by the uniqueness of information presented herein—much of which I was not aware of even after 35 years in the industry, 19 as a CEO. Glaess brings our industry to life with his artfully stated points, "strange but true" detail, little known factoids, the subtle and sometimes not so subtle humorous asides. Cover to cover it is interesting stuff, interestingly told. Don't miss it."

—MARK VOGT, retired CEO of Wright-Hennepin
Cooperative Electric Association

"Mark Glaess is the best-read cooperative leader I have ever met. Now, he has joined the ranks of esteemed authors with a thought-provoking and deeply researched book about the rural electric program. It's an essential read for those interested in the past and future of the one of the greatest programs ever created."

—TED CASE, CEO of the Oregon Rural Electric Association
and author of *Power Plays and Poles, Wires and War*

Aspire
to Better

Aspire
to Better

The 21st Century Electric Cooperative

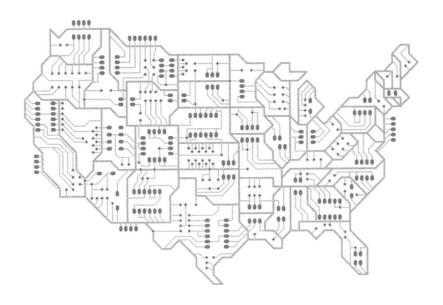

MARK GLAESS

Book design services provided by Indigo: Editing, Design, and More. Cover and interior design by Vinnie Kinsella.

ISBN: 978-0-578-30236-2

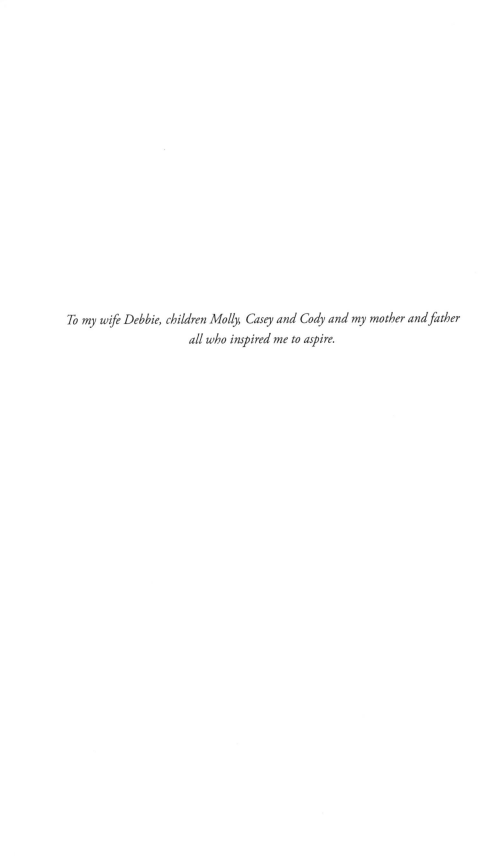

To my wife Debbie, children Molly, Casey and Cody and my mother and father all who inspired me to aspire.

Contents

Introduction

Faith is like electricity. You can't see it, but you can see the light

F aith is like electricity. You can't see electricity but you can see the light. Time doesn't always provide an explanation for past events. Like how my grandpa, Arnold Glaess, happened to play golf with the poet, Robert Frost. That must have been around 1925 or 1926. Or why my grandpa, a Lutheran schoolteacher in Harbor Beach, Michigan, was sufficiently acquainted with Henry Ford to loan the wallet-less automaker money to return to Detroit. Or how my grandma, Vincenta, came to make clothes for Frank William Murphy's children. Murphy, a resident of Harbor Beach, was a Michigan governor who was appointed to the Supreme Court by Franklin Roosevelt. We do know, however, from my Grandma, that she also made clothes for Thomas Alva Edison's children.

On her one hundredth birthday in 2002, Vincenta told her grandson, who then worked in the electric cooperative vineyards, that of all the inventions she witnessed—from airplanes to the Internet—it was electricity that she found to be the greatest. There's many ideas about that observation. Here's mine, which might not be yours, but bear with me, it's all intended to be instructive or illuminating which, in any event, produces light.

In 1943, New Hampshire Electric was credited for making possible the transmission of an NBC program on democracy to the rural reaches in the Granite State.[1] New Hampshire Electric, now an 84,000 member co-op, was the beneficiary of the 1935 Rural Electrification Administration which was responsible for financing the creation of some 850 electric co-ops in forty-eight states. Nearly a half-century later, one of those co-ops, the Ramsey, Minnesota-based Connexus Energy, provided the current to transmit the twenty-sixth Super Bowl seen by some 120 million views worldwide. In between those events, there's a rich history affecting the lives of some 43 million Americans

1

and, by extension, another 160 million worldwide. That story starts in the first chapter and first verse of Genesis which makes short order of God's creation of the heavens and the earth. The next job after that was light. Millenniums later, Edison found the right filament in 1880 to illuminate urban America.[2] It would be another fifty-six years before rural America set aside kerosene lamps for those they envied in Sears catalogues.

In the early 1930s, envy was about the only spendable commodity. A 1962 book by Harold Severson entitled, *The Night They Turned on the Lights*, recounted the grim reality of Minnesota's rural areas looking to gain sufficient customers to entice the Rural Electrification Administration, or REA, to lend them the funds needed to purchase poles and wire. Attendees at local church events organized by the Farm Bureau, or local extension agents, mumbled that, "Electricity was for city people and kerosene lamps for rural people." North Star Electric, which abuts Canada, saw the locals sighing that, "Prospects were dim, even REA said so." Anoka County residents, who later would form Anoka Electric, the predecessor of the Super Bowl-providing Connexus Energy, were equally glum noting, "It was not a favorable year for starting anything, let alone an electric co-op."[3]

The farmers weren't wrong. Authors Ridley Scott and Richard Rudolph recount in *Power Struggles* that farm income averaged $1800 a year and that wheat was selling for eighty cents a bushel. In 1935, only 11 percent of rural America had electricity and the cost to bring it was enormously expensive as it was $2000–$3000 per mile for line extensions from one of the private power companies.[4]

In what's likely the best historical account of the REA comes from the pages of *The Next Greatest Thing*, authored by Patrick Dahl and Dick Pence in 1984 to commemorate the fiftieth anniversary of the REA. The following is an account of how, and why, electric cooperatives were regarded as the next greatest thing.[5]

"He tried for years to get electricity to his farm. He saw how hard his wife worked without electricity. She had to haul water, put hot coals in the iron, not only cook over a wood stove, but likely had to chop it as well. He saw that his children didn't have the same educational opportunities of their city cousins, all because they didn't have electricity. Finally, he made the decision to talk to the local power manager to see how much it would cost to extend electricity to his Tennessee Farm. Cost wasn't necessarily an issue, location was, that power official said. If you want it, he told the farmer, you'll have to move your farm to where our poles are located.[6]

"Trudging home, the farmer made up his mind and told his family upon his arrival his plans. 'We're going to move the farms so we can get electricity.' The next day he went to town and told the power guy his decision only to be told not to bother. If he moved his farm to get lights, then others would do so and that just wouldn't work out for the power company."

Robert Caro wrote about how much rural electrification meant to the Hill Country of Lyndon Baines Johnson and it is the second installment of his LBJ quadrilogy entitled, *The Path to Power*. In the chapter entitled Sad Irons, Caro describes how hard the Hill Country women had to work hauling water, cooking over wood stoves, and canning vegetables with the lack of refrigeration, all "because there was no electricity…"[7]

In 1924, Franklin Roosevelt began visiting Warm Springs seeking rejuvenation in the area's famous hot springs for his legs stricken by polio. That pastoral Georgia town would be known as FDR's Little White House and would be the inspiration for the Rural Electrification Administration or REA. According to lore, Roosevelt said the light bill he received for his little cottage was four times what he paid at Hyde Park, New York. That rate difference, FDR asserted, "started my long study of proper utility charges for electricity and the whole subject of getting electricity into farm homes throughout the United States."[8]

The electricity task was first offered to private power companies to serve rural America and, as the Tennessee farmer would later learn, they largely refused, saying either there was no money to be made or that farmers didn't need electrification. Harold Ickes, then Secretary of the Interior, when presented with opportunities for the private power companies to extend power to rural areas, responded, "I'll have nothing to do with those sons-of-bitches."[9] What then ensued was the idea of using the cooperative model, much in use among farmers, for electrification. Roosevelt did so by creating the REA with his Executive Order 7037 in 1935 followed a year later by Congressional approval led by Nebraska Senator George Norris and Mississippi Representative John Rankin.

In 1935, 10.9 percent or 744,000 farm and rural residents had electricity. Urban America did a bit better: 62 million or 57.3 percent.[10] Ten years later, 90 percent of rural America had the joy of juice and the cost to extend a mile of line decreased from $3000 per mile to $600.[11] Which brings us back to that Tennessean. In anticipation of when the co-op would finally bring electricity to his home, he wired the house and barn for lights and later took his family up a small hill to see those lights penetrate the darkness. The following day, a Sunday, saw the farmer in church which afforded an opportunity for the parishioners to give testimony of their faith. The farmer rose and made this observation, "Brothers and sisters, I want to tell you this. The greatest thing on earth is to have the love of Jesus in your heart and the next greatest thing is to have electricity in your house."[12]

Roosevelt, who backed the idea of rural electrification as part of the New Deal, did so as one of many programs to lift the country out of the depression and he made this observation, "The test of our progress is not whether we add more to the abundance of those who have much; it is whether we provide enough for those who have too little."[13]

In his 1960 classic, *The Age of Roosevelt: The Politics of Upheaval*, historian Arthur M. Schlesinger portrayed utility companies as uneager and unwilling to electrify rural America. When describing the REA created in 1935, however, he wrote, "No single public agency ever so enriched and brightened the quality of rural living."[14] Author William Leuchtenburg observed that "perhaps no single act of the Roosevelt years changed more directly the way people lived than the President's creation of the Rural Electrification Administration."[15] *Power Plays*, a book authored by Oregon Rural Electric Cooperative Association CEO, Ted Case, recounted when Lyndon Johnson was asked what his most important contribution was. He could have cited any of the Great Society programs, including Medicare and the voting rights act, but chose instead, "Bringing electricity to the Hill Country of Texas."[16]

According to the US Senate Historian, Nebraska's George Norris is the man many consider history's greatest United States senator. Norris, hailing from McCook, Nebraska, served in the Senate for thirty years from 1913 until 1943 and had this to say about legislation that created the REA. "REA will have made one of the greatest contributions toward the improvement of farms that that could possibly be imagined."[17]

Of course, the history of the REA and the nearly 850 co-ops that program has spawned is closing on ninety years. In 2013, the National Rural Electric Cooperative Association, or NRECA, the national trade association for most of those purveyors of the next greatest thing, attempted to answer the question, "Can we do it again." That inquiry was posed by Mike Williams, the CEO of the Texas Electric Cooperative Association which, in turn, created the 21st Century Committee devoted to answering that very question.[18]

It is now years since Williams and company answered that question. Except, in that case, what became of the recommendations of the committee which produced one of the co-op's most important documents since Morris Cooke outlined the necessity for rural electrification in a memo that he famously said could be read in twelve minutes?

Joining me for this book is Jason Makansi, himself a celebrated author of several books including *Painting by Numbers, The Carbon IRA and Your Utility,* and a book entitled, *Lights Out* published in 2007 which saw any number of state trade co-op associations invite Jason to expand upon his then electric vision. Jason also at one time was the editor of Power Magazine, the founder of Pearl Street, Inc., and a consultant on numerous energy-related concerns including storage. Jason's views on developing a carbon Individual Retirement Account add a patina to my book.

Me? I've worked with different statewides including as the Legislative Director for the Nebraska Rural Electric Association. I was the guy Oregon hired to form the Oregon Rural Electric Cooperative Association and later was the fourth CEO of the Minnesota Rural Electric Association. I also had a stint on the National Rural Telecommunications Board of Directors for nine years. Which brings two caveats: Forbes Magazine on January 24, 2017 featured an article by Mark Murphy who opined on the Dunning-Kruger effect. Here's Murphy's salient points.

"If you've ever dealt with someone whose performance stinks, and they're not only clueless that their performance stinks, but they're confident that their performance is good, you likely saw the Dunning-Kruger effect in action. Coined in 1999 by then-Cornell psychologists, David Dunning and Justin

Kruger, the eponymous Dunning-Kruger effect is a cognitive bias whereby people who are incompetent at something are unable to recognize their own incompetence. And not only do they fail to recognize their incompetence, they're also likely to feel confident that they actually are competent."[19]

The second, however, is instructive. Malcom Gladwell, latest book is entitled: "The Bomber Mafia." You should read it. On page 32, Gladwell makes this observation[20]: "Conversations starts to seed a revolution," or in this case, becoming a 21st Century cooperative.

With both caveats in mind, in the following pages we'll recount how co-ops have fared in answering the question, "Can we do it again," along with travels down the travails that have defined the electricity industry including the seemingly lost historical document written in 2013.

CHAPTER 1

The Electric Cooperative Purpose

I t must have been in the early months of 1935 that Morris Cooke made the case for rural electrification in a memo entitled, The 12 Minutes.[1] That period turns out to be the time of the drum solo, In-A-Gadda-Da-Vida, the mandatory 1968 prom song by Iron Butterfly.[2] It was also when President Roosevelt created the REA on May 11, 1935 with Executive Order No. 7037. Roosevelt was able to do that under powers granted by the Emergency Relief Appropriation Act of 1935.[3] The goal of the REA was to bring electricity to America's rural areas which at that time saw light in about 3 percent of those areas.[4]

At first, and it is the underpinning of REA's continued social mission, the agency was "initially expected to provide direct relief to the nation's unemployed." That job creation was shelved (but would loom large years later) when very few of the unemployed in rural areas had the needed electrical trade skills.[5]

A year later in May 1936, Congress passed Public Law 74–605, best known as the REA Act authored by Nebraska US Senator George Norris and Mississippi Congressman John Rankin. Initially, REA was an independent agency with a large amount of latitude given to it. In 1939, the REA was made a part of the United States Department of Agriculture.[6] Today, it's known as the Rural Utilities Service or RUS.

Fittingly, the REA Act now hangs in NRECA headquarters alongside portraits of those who mattered including Franklin Delano Roosevelt. One incorporator of the 1936 REA Act is the name of a rural electric system in Nebraska and it is called the Norris Public Power District. Norris PPD serves Seward County where I once lived. Any memorialization of John Rankin dissipated based on the overt racial views of Mississippians including legislative proposals to outlaw interracial marriages and support for incarcerating

Japanese-American citizens in concentration camps following the bombing of Pearl Harbor. Despite Rankin's odious views, legislation he sponsored lifted all races out of poverty because of the GI Bill, the REA Act, and the Tennessee Valley Act which provides energy to about 150 co-op and municipal-owned utilities. Imperfect men underscore the belief that "God works in mysterious ways" which, by the way, isn't biblical and thus avoids a theological footnote. But still.

In May of 1985, the US Post Office issued a fiftieth anniversary stamp commemorating the Rural Electrification Act. Frank Gallant was one of the finest chroniclers of rural electrification while he was the editor of the NRECA monthly publication entitled RE Magazine. RE stood for Rural Electrification. Gallant noted in the May 2020 issue that the stamp's unveiling in May 1985 attracted 1,500 people to Madison, South Dakota.[7] Can there be a greater tribute to a twelve minutes to read memo—faster to read, perhaps, if you're Evelyn Wood—than a commemorative stamp to celebrate our collective beginning?

The Morris Cooke memo is the canon for electric cooperatives. Close behind was an effort begun in 1967 when the co-ops were running short of REA money which was then an appropriated amount of $300 million at 2 percent. In response to the cash call, NRECA formed the snappily named Long-Range Study Committee to essentially develop a co-op bank since, history repeating itself, no one else wanted to risk lending huge amounts of dough to co-ops and G&Ts.[8] Thirty representatives from distribution systems, generation and transmission cooperatives (G&Ts), and statewide associations representing all NRECA regions met to calculate the mechanics of a cooperatively owned and controlled banking system. J. K. Smith, longtime general manager of the Kentucky Association of Electric Cooperatives, chaired the group. Smith would be selected as the first CEO of the organization known as the National Rural Utilities Cooperative Finance Corporation[9] or CFC as it's known on logoed golf balls scattered in the woods across America.

There were 512 co-ops that would become the original incorporators of a co-op bank in 1969 and each contributed $1000 in seed money. Statewides contributed $200 and, not for the first time, complained about that cost.[10] Over a half century later, CFC is a $27 billion bank owned by co-ops and is more than living up to its motto, "There's more where that came from." A later chapter will cover exactly what *more* means.

You can point to succeeding reports on governance, capital credits, and acquiring the RUS loan program from the always blue ribbon commission of the all-things electric cooperative. However, in the trilogy of the reports most critical to furthering rural electrification and deeper investment in the cooperative principles, is the report of the NRECA 21st Century Committee Report entitled, The Electric Cooperative Purpose. (https://www.cooperative.com/maps-facts-figures/Documents/Secure/21stCenturyFinalReport.pdf)[11]

Texas Electric Cooperative, the largest statewide in the nation, includes seventy-five co-ops serving over three million Texans. The President and CEO is the impressive Mike Williams who took control of that statewide in 1993 from the legendary Jim Morris who once worked for LBJ's radio station and who had to get Johnson's permission to run TEC. TEC is an unusual statewide because it also offers a full line of utility supplies and services, including utility poles, through its manufacturing and distribution services in addition to government affairs and loss control services. TEC was a $13 million venture when Williams left his job minding Texas municipal-owned utilities to helm TEC. Under Williams, TEC now counts a staggering $300 million in revenues.

While the TEC electric cooperative program was well past the Y2K scare, Williams asked the simple but astonishing question, "Can we do it again?" That inquiry led then NRECA CEO, Glenn English, to convene a committee, as Williams notes in the Chairman's letter, "to assess the future of electric cooperatives and articulate the vision that ensures that electric cooperatives are successful and sustainable in the coming years." You really should read that again, particularly given the fact that from 1955 to 2017 only sixty remain among the Fortune 500 companies listed during that time.[12] The efforts of Williams and the Committee were designed for longevity.

Here are ten salient points from the sixty-one recommendations in that 2013 report:[13]

1. A clearly defined and understood purpose allows a business to operate from its core and holds the enterprise steady during times of uncertainty.

2. As member-owned businesses, cooperatives have a unique self-help role in the American economy that distinguishes them from other private businesses, charity, and government.

3. The scope of cooperative member-owner empowerment extends from the simplest acts of participation such as voting in cooperative elections, participation in member advisory committees, being elected to the cooperative board, and extensive involvement in projects to improve member and community quality of life.

4. The national demographic of cooperative members is looking more and more like that of the nation as a whole with the fastest growth in metropolitan areas and showing the same trends toward an older and more culturally-diverse population.

5. Research shows that a critical mass of around 15 percent of loyal and engaged member-owners is a tipping point to energize the larger membership.

6. Direct experiences with their cooperative will instill in members a sense of ownership that forms the basis for trust and loyalty.

7. Electric cooperatives are embedded in their communities and can build on their business relationships to empower members and pursue opportunities for community enrichment.

8. Distribution cooperatives will need enhanced financial, technological, and organizational capabilities to meet the challenges and opportunities of the emerging consumer-centric electricity and energy market of the twenty-first century.

9. While today cooperatives are still considered to be trusted advisors for their members, if the cooperatives cannot meet the challenges of the new energy marketplace, third parties could move in to fill the void.

10. The cooperative program is a natural laboratory that contains emerging knowledge and innovations occurring across the cooperative landscape.

The 2013 report is a remarkable document (although, for some unexplained reason, NRECA no longer features the report in its website). Much hoopla was given at the time along with the equivalent of a meter lamp given to Williams to thank him for his efforts. Yet, the tenets of that report have not resonated across the years as they should. Ten recommendations were noted. Here's one example of how they could play out. Some time ago, the Minnesota-based Connexus Energy received an application for service from an adult bookstore. Management noted the request and reported the co-op's area-wide service requirement necessitated energizing that particular library. The Board nonetheless questioned the application, perhaps thinking a site visit was necessary before moving on to the checks written list. Today, there exists an even bigger opportunity that once was equated with lascivious literature.

The Williams report[14] suggests cooperative engagement to "find opportunities to work face to face with groups of their members." Given that sensible exhortation, and the co-op's universal embrace of load building that is second only to co-op directors at CFC's hosted bar, it is possible they should pursue marijuana loads. According to Governing Magazine, thirty-four states either allow recreational use of cannabis, or with a doctor's prescription, and that includes South Dakota and Oklahoma.[15]

Cannabis represents an enormous load. Inland Power and Light discovered soon after the State of Washington legalized pot that their load grew by over 20 MW. Twenty-four-hour loads are foreign to most co-ops that generally deal with seasonal loads like irrigation or grain drying that cause rate issues with their G&Ts. Pot, on the other hand, needs constant kWh tending, if not monitoring, those are things a co-op excels in along with the knowledge of zoning requirements and locations for suitable pot farming. Or not, given that marijuana continues to be classified as a Schedule 1 narcotic. That likely means the co-op won't be using the Rural Development Loan and Grant program or REDLG[16] to entice loads and they won't see RUS financing substations to serve those loads and perhaps causing the CFC Regional VP to suggest using internal funds to serve marijuana purveyors and be on the lookout for membership questions.

Then again, wasn't there a similar reaction years ago when tribes began to build casinos, upsetting some directors who showed a lack of affinity for American Indians. That, in turn, prompted some to cite the First Timothy admonition about the love of money and all that. Today, co-ops serve some

250 tribes, many who have casinos, representing a great load. An improved load factor has an equalizing effect leading to the embrace and support of casinos if, for no other reason, the famous buffets.

Look at recommendation number 4[17] which states, "The national demographic of cooperative members is looking more and more like those of the nation as a whole," not, we add, the nation as aged, largely white, and mostly male co-op directors may see it. While area-wide coverage fortunately doesn't allow co-ops to discriminate who they serve or not serve, the ethic that the 21st Century Committee posits is, "Find opportunities." That's not only for loads but for governance, power supply, mergers, providing for the least of them, forming new co-ops, and cooperative evangelism among the next chapters attempting to answer the multifaceted question, "Can we do it again?"

It is a mystery why the document wasn't the basis for education seminars and that NRECA's Education and Conferences didn't embrace the concept. As an aside, that department surely must rank as the best among the thousands of trade association education departments for the length and breadth of the subjects covered, making the absence of teaching the tenets of that seminal report all the more puzzling. I will address what that course might look like later in this book.

For now, the next chapter is on co-op largesse, reflecting the Committee's observation that on average co-ops are involved in thirty-one "separate community-based activities.[18] As Willy Wonka was wont to say, "So shines a good deed in a weary world."[19]

Chapter 2

We're the Helpers

I n 1989, Tom Upshaw wondered how his co-op could put its best face forward for the municipal areas it served in order to keep the IOUs out. Upshaw said the idea of rounding up customers' electric bills to assist those in need came to him at 4:00 a.m. one morning and it's unusual because that's usually when management hears about outages. Upshaw, then the CEO of the South Carolina-based Palmetto Electric, whose service area included Hilton Head or the best of customers, also served hard pockets of poverty. Upshaw said the key focus of the program is to "help people out of rough spots...to help them out of that emergency or hole that they're in at that particular point in time."

What accounts for the generous spirit endemic to most co-op practices and found in countless examples of their community sharing and giving? The spirit of the electric co-op seems to adhere to biblical tenets as well as the best social initiatives to help those in need. That impetus has offered creative and lucrative help over the last several decades. Berl Davis, now CEO of Palmetto Electric, reports nearly 350 co-ops in thirty-nine states have implemented a roundup program. Davis said an estimated $250 million has been raised since Upshaw got his middle-of-the-night inspiration. Subsequently, many thousands have received assistance to help them through life's rough spots.

In the early 1990s, Freeborn-Mower electric co-op located in Albert Lea, Minnesota, invited local swells and the media to meet the owners of businesses assisted by the Rural Economic Development Loan and Grant Program or REDLG. One woman stepped forward to tell the assembly that without the co-op loaning money to help the company that hired her, she'd still be on welfare. REDLG was a creation of Rich LaRochelle who first conceived the economic development program while toiling for RUS. Later, he would be

Government Affairs Director for NRECA and then someone special at CFC. Rich said REDLG was created to address the economic downturn in rural America. That Grant and Loan Program has lent or given over $900 million and, by NRECA's calculation, has created or saved over 76,000 jobs since 1989. Isn't that the blessing the Beatitudes promised to the poor?

In 1962, NRECA's first Manager, Clyde Ellis, signed an inaugural cooperative agreement with the US Agency for International Development, with President Kennedy in attendance, to create an electric co-op in Bolivia. Today, NRECA's International Program counts 250 electric cooperatives serving an astonishing 121 million members.[1] There are 350 co-ops that together have donated an average of $1.2 million annually and sent some sixty line workers every year. Perhaps that astonishing and nearly worldwide electrification came from the advice from the Book of James[2] combining faith with good so that great works would illuminate the world.

Moreau Grand EC is located in Timber which is characteristic of much of South Dakota—few folks per mile of line. It's a bit better after that co-op, led by Melissa Mahler in the early 1990s, participated in a Habitat for Humanity building blitz. That was well before Extreme Makeover: Home Edition aired. Jeff Nelson, then CEO of East River Electric recalled that 3000 volunteers, including former President Jimmy Carter and First Lady Roselyn Carter, built thirty homes in thirty days. Those homes were located in the co-op service area. Moreau Grand EC supplied the electric connection proving that, yes, Moreau Grande juice is the next greatest thing.

One inspiration for "This little light of mine, I'm going to let it shine" is said to be from the book of Matthew 5:16[3] which extols letting your light shine on your good works. Look no further than the illumination provided by 2021's 1600 high school-age students who attended the NRECA Youth Tour.[4] Texas Senator Lyndon Johnson inspired NRECA to do that when he suggested at a 1957 national meeting that, "If one thing comes out of this meeting, it will be sending youngsters to the national capital where they can actually see what the flag stands for and represents." Some 50,000 mostly rural youngsters have received showers of patriotism, among them Apple CEO Tim Cook who was sponsored by Alabama-based Baldwin County in 1977.

Another notable edict is, "God helps those who help themselves." Well, that's not biblical but helping others is reminiscent of the Good Samaritan and is represented by the Minnesota Rural Electric Association. In 2006, that Statewide hosted a golf tournament to raise money for three burn centers. The striking Statewide CEO, Darrick Moe, whose golf handicap includes a greens fee restraining order, reports that The Burn Center Open has raised close to $300,000 since its inception. Connexus Energy generally hires scratch golfers on a one-day contract to win that event which, by the way, is not considered in the next greatest thing category.[5]

It was Ben Franklin who is attributed with the idea that God kicks the goods over to the DIY enthusiasts.[6] So it is with co-ops nationally and they contribute to storm-stricken co-ops leveled by hurricanes Sandy, Katrina, and Rita—floods that rivaled those navigated by Noah. For the Midwest, it also includes ice crashing down on hundreds of miles of aluminum conductors and tornadoes sucking up infrastructure having the temerity to stand in their way. Co-ops understand the difficulty of maintaining service-institutionalized mutual aid agreements. When the damage is done, co-op vehicles of all colors—well, mostly yellow—create their own tent cities while repairing many homes left electrically bereft. According to Billy Gibson, then Communications Director for the Louisiana Statewide, co-ops poured over $2.3 million in assistance following Rita and, in particular, he cited CFC, CoBank, and Basin Electric—a North Dakota-based G&T located 1,550 miles away. Perhaps the idea was put best, however, in Matthew 7:25: "The rain came down, the streams rose, and the winds blew and beat against that house; yet it did not fall because it had its foundation on the rock."[7] Co-ops have always tended to hew to that godly rock.

Then there is the Honor Flight. The South Carolina Statewide under the inspired leadership of CEO, Mike Couick, started that program in 2013 for flying WW II veterans to visit the memorial dedicated in Washington to the Greatest Generation which lost 450,000 in the cause of freedom. The Statewide raised $60,000 to fly eighty-five veterans. One veteran said, "If I don't live another day, this will be the most wonderful day of my life."[8]

The Book of Proverbs is a chatty number offering observation and advice including this sample: "The heart of the discerning acquires knowledge, for

15

the ears of the wise seek it out."[9] The Oregon Statewide CEO, Ted Case, himself a literate author of two books, *Power Plays* and *Poles, Wires and War*, reports that the Oregon Trail Electric Cooperative partners with the Dolly Parton Imagination Library[10] which provides free books to children from birth to five years. The organization has 3,000 books donated annually including, presumably, "Good Night Moon."[11]

Cooperatives are supposed to return patronage to their members. Still, the $15 billion repatriated since 1990, as told by NRECA's statistic department's David Oliver and Madelyn Roche, is astonishing and done without asking but instead answering, "What's in your wallet?" Then there's unclaimed capital credits. While we don't know how many millions of dollars that represents, thousands of kids whose educational pursuits have been funded with that American currency have a clear idea of its importance.

Texas Electric Cooperative CEO, Mike Williams, again asked the question as to why co-ops were created in the first place. The Twenty-First Century co-op study, chaired by the magnetic Williams in 2013, said—and you'll want to take note of it—that it was to improve the lives of the members.

It was Franklin Delano Roosevelt who backed the idea of rural electrification. Roosevelt, the architect of so many programs to lift the country out of the depression, made this observation, "We have always held to the hope, the belief, and the conviction that there is a better life, a better world, beyond the horizon."[12]

Rightfully, co-ops will cite the seventh cooperative principle, concern for community, as a rationale for their compassion. In the end, perhaps it's what Mr. Rogers, of the PBS program Mr. Roger's Neighborhood, learned as a boy when confronted with scary news. His mom, Rogers recalled, would say, "Look for the helpers."[13] That's who we are. It's who we've always been. It's what our industry is founded upon. We're the helpers.

One conservative columnist, George Will, commented on "the increase in American happiness wrought by rural electrification."[14]

Chapter 3

RUS: Providing for the Least of Them

You can check your Gideon Bible, perhaps swiped from the last out-of-town statewide meeting, to enumerate any number of gospel passages that describe the blessing that is the Rural Utilities Service or RUS. For my money, which aptly describes the lending agency, you might look at Matthew 25:40 which recounts the Sermon on the Mount and particularly speaks of the "least of them."[1] That defines rural America. Here's how the USDA described the urban-rural income split in 2017: "Since 2007, rural median income has averaged 25 percent below the urban median."[2]

Measuring anything starts at first with the recognition of without or absence. Think again of the millions of largely rural Americans who toiled without the munificence of electricity. Caro, once again, said it best, "Because there was no electricity, one gains yet again another appreciation for what REA and its successor agency, RUS, have meant to rural America."[3] Here's a story that underscores what REA meant.

Bob Partridge, who succeeded Clyde Ellis as the CEO of NRECA, joined REA after World War II and rose to be the Assistant Chief for the Division of Program Analysis from 1946 until 1954. So important was REA to some Members of Congress that Partridge told the story that then Congressman Lyndon Baines Johnson stood over his shoulder in an effort to speed his loan approval for Hill Country electric cooperatives. According to Robert Caro's book entitled, *The Years of Lyndon Johnson: The Path to Power*, President Roosevelt offered Johnson the job as Administrator of the REA "principally because it indicated the strength of the impression Johnson had made on Roosevelt once he got the chance to spend time with him. The director-ship of a nationwide agency, particularly one as fast-growing and politically important as REA, was not the kind of job offered to many men still short of their thirty-first birthday."[4] Others, however, didn't agree including one unlikely opponent.

The 1993 NRECA Legislative Conference was held when Bill Clinton presented his inaugural State of the Union speech. Co-op attendees had reason to see the former Arkansas governor as a friend of the co-ops if for no other reason than that Clinton credited then Arkansas Statewide Manager, Carl Whillock, for helping him to win election as Governor in Arkansas in 1983 after Clinton lost the Governorship in 1981.

Despite Whillock's tutelage, or the political prominence of the Arkansas co-ops, or simply the immutable law that no good deed goes unpunished, Clinton told the millions of viewers of his intent to end subsidized loans for electric cooperatives which he labeled as a "beloved program of the United States." That was a puzzling rejoinder to a program with a cost to the government, if measured in a year, that amounted to just a few minutes over 365 days. That was not the first attempt to end the insured loan program.[5]

Dwight Eisenhower, was antithetical to REA as was his Vice President, Richard Nixon. When Nixon became President, he took aim at the program co-ops soon after his Christmas cheer faded in 1972. Nixon's New Year's resolution directed the US Department of Agriculture to deny funds already authorized by Congress for the Rural Electrification Administration's upcoming fiscal year and he then terminated the agency's direct loan program. For thirty-six years, that program had enabled the REA to offer loans to co-ops at 2 percent interest. NRECA would accede to a 5 percent loan program but hardship systems, largely based on density, could continue to borrow funds at 2 percent.

Twenty-one years later, Clinton's announcement resulted in the offering of three different rate structures, a compromise engineered by Whillock.[6]

- Interest rates increased from 2 percent to 5 percent for hardship systems with rates 20 percent higher than neighboring utilities. That ended in 2013.
- Rates equal to the cost of municipal loans were capped at 7 percent and that ended in 2008.
- Loans at the government cost of money plus one-eighth of 1 percent.

The recounting of RUS loans that are now available for, well, practically anything for rural America, and covering the quality of water to the speed of the internet, shows that the political interest in disabling that agency has largely diminished. Republican Administrations, usually hostile to a lending program that was thought to provide co-ops with a competitive balance against IOUs, saw successive Presidents like George Bush and then Clinton, Obama, Trump, and now President Biden largely adding to the portfolio of RUS and particularly for broadband. Former RUS Administrator, Chris McLean, posed the theoretical question of "what would rural America be if they didn't have affordable electricity, clean water, and high-speed internet largely financed through RUS?" McLean could have added that RUS is now scored, in budget parlance, as a negative appropriation. That means the money RUS makes off of loans to co-ops through the Federal Financing Bank carries a one-eighth of 1 percent fee which makes RUS one of the few federal programs that makes money for the government and that is one reason to explain RUS's foray into energy conservation.[7]

- The Rural Energy Savings Program or RESP was designed to provide energy efficiency loans.
- The Energy Efficiency and Conservation Loan Program or EECLP was designed in part to allow co-ops to provide low-interest loans to its membership for energy efficiency measures behind the meter and paid monthly through electric bills.
- EECLP was particularly popular for the installation of ground source heat pumps and demand-side management investments.
- Distributed generation loans are made to either co-ops wishing to own or operate the project or to renewable energy developers serving in rural areas. The loan requires a minimum 25 percent cash equity by the co-op or developer and the output is 100 percent subscribed by rural residents. Distributed energy loans are likely the financing source for solar gardens operated by co-ops.
- High Energy Cost loans are made to households whose energy cost exceeds 275 percent of the national average (averaging about 35 cents/kWh). That program is largely directed at tribes and Alaskan

villages and it is to be used for storage tanks to hold diesel, hydro development, backup generators, and energy savings appliances.

- The Rural Business Service, a division of RUS, also offers the REDLG loan program and the Rural Energy for America Program or REAP. The latter is designed to assist agricultural producers.

For those not grasping the largesse that could be used by co-ops, or appreciative of bullet points, $600 million has been appropriated for the Rural Energy for America Program. Applicants—and they could be the co-op or their competitors—can cage 25 percent of a project cost in grants, or free dough, and the remainder in a guaranteed loan program. Here's what that project financing did in several locations in Iowa as noted in a 2018 CleanTechnica article:[8]

- Farmers Saving Bank in Wever, Iowa is using a $16,062 REAP grant to help purchase and install solar array panels.
- B&A Mallory Corporation in Stuart is using a $15,873 REAP grant to help purchase and install six refrigeration units and a six-horse-power compressor for a locally owned grocery store.
- Riley Industrial Painting, Inc. in Burlington is using a $5,995 REAP grant to replace current lighting fixtures with LED fixtures that use less energy.
- Duwa's Auction Service LLC in Wellman is using a $13,280 REAP grant to help purchase and install a solar array panel.

According to the USDA, the Energy Efficiency and Conservation Loan Program, awkwardly known as EECLP, funded these cool projects:[9]

- USDA awarded a $6 million EECLP loan to North Carolina's Roanoke Electric Membership Corporation to finance improvements to HVAC systems, replace appliances, and build envelope improvements for about 200 residential energy efficiency upgrades per year over the next four years.
- USDA provided the North Arkansas Electric Cooperative with a $4.6 million loan to fund geothermal and air source installations,

energy efficiency lightning, and weatherization measures including Energy Star® windows and doors, insulation, and efficient water heaters and roofing. Financing will reduce energy costs for consumers and improve the utility services.

There are many more programs administered under the Rural Business Service. If you are seeking to answer the 21st Century Committee's key question, "Can we do it again," you will find these programs of value for retaining a co-op's legacy of relevance:[10]

- Business and Industry Loan Guarantees underwrites a percentage of loans for private businesses up to $25 million.
- The Intermediary Relending Program provides 1 percent interest loans to co-ops for revolving loan funds to assist local businesses.
- Rural Business Development Grants ranging from $10,000 to $500,000 lead to the development or expansion of small private businesses located in Rural 1 areas.
- The Rural Business Investments Program forms venture capital organizations to fulfill the capital needs of rural areas.
- REDLG, or the Rural Economic Development Loan and Grant program, is now capped at $1.2 million which has proven to be among the most popular of the Rural Business offerings.
- Rural Microentreprenueur Assistance Program supports cool new rural start-ups.
- Value Added Producer Grants are made to farmers and ranchers who have an innovative plan to make their produce even more valuable.
- Community Facilities Programs provides funding for infrastructure for everything from housing to health care to fire and rescue that are designed to improve the quality of life for rural America or, said another way, why electric co-ops exist.

There's more American currency available through RUS, the Rural Utility Service, and the Water and Environmental Service. Undrinkable water exposed what many considered to be environmental racism in Flint, Michigan when that city switched from the Detroit River to the highly corrosive Flint River for water supply which included high levels of lead. Tainted water is a concern for rural areas particularly for tribes, some 250 of which are served by co-ops. Here's a listing of programs that co-ops can avail in order to ensure that water remains heaven-sent to their members.[10]

- Circuit Rider Program provides consulting services to small water projects
- Emergency Community Water Assistance Grants
- Grants for Rural and Native Alaskan Villages for, among other things, to remedy adverse sanitation conditions
- Household Water Well System Grants
- Individual Water & Wastewater Grants for up to $3,500 to install plumbing for homes in unserved rural areas
- SEARCH - Special Evaluation Assistance for Rural Communities and Households
- Solid Waste Management Grants
- Water & Waste Disposal Grants to Alleviate Health Risks on Tribal Lands and Colonias which are rural communities within the US-Mexico border region that lack adequate water, sewer, and decent housing or a combination of all three
- Water & Waste Disposal Loans & Grants
- Water & Waste Disposal Loan Guarantees
- Water & Waste Disposal Predevelopment Planning Grants
- Water & Waste Disposal Technical Assistance & Training Grants

Boom. A catalogue of goods the co-op can tap to do Sermon on the Mount stuff. Best of all, RUS has field representatives scattered all over to assist a co-op in showing, in the most demonstrative way possible, that it cares for its members. In its eighty-fifth year, the RUS electric program has a loan portfolio of $45 billon.

Well before FDR had his Warm Springs epiphany, a Nebraska Congressman by the name of William Jennings Bryan ran for President in 1896 and had this to say, known as the Cross of Gold speech:[11]

"Burn down your cities and leave our farms, and your cities will spring up again as if by magic. But destroy our farms and the grass will grow in the streets of every city in the country."

That is what RUS spawned. Both a vital rural area and a wellspring of urban centers. In the long, and distinguished list of contributors to the 21st Century Committee, no one from RUS was mentioned. In fact, the report largely omitted any reference to the agency responsible for lighting rural America. If there is fault to be found in what turned out to be one of the great documents for electric cooperatives, the absence of the agency that brought the great stuff to rural America which historians have ranked as the great asset to America's far-flung reaches and ahead of the tractor and fertilizer, then that is it.

Beside all that, REA also was prescient all those years ago about governance. More on that in the next chapter.

Chapter 4

7 Deadly Sins Supersede

the 7 Cooperative Principles

In August of 2015, Washington Post reporter, Chris Ingraham, investigated a USDA index on the best and worst places to live.[1] Ventura County, home to an agreeable climate and grapes far outpaced the worst place according to Ingraham's USDA findings which was Red Lake County, Minnesota. That county is also home to Red Lake Electric Cooperative. Each month, Red Lake Electric sends their 4,316 members a newsletter called Volts and Jolts[2] which describes the goings-on in their co-op. One edition found then new Manager, Stephanie Johnson, introducing herself and noting that she once was an accountant for Roseau Electric whose members include the late NRECA CEO, Congressman, and USDA Secretary Bob Bergland. The chatty newsletter also introduced summer help and had pictures of the twenty-one co-op members who visited the Milton R. Young coal-based generation located near Center, North Dakota which was named for the six-term Senator who was a particular pal of co-ops. Also featured were pictures of twenty-two high school soon-to-be seniors who were awarded $500 scholarships funded largely by unclaimed capital credits.

Cooperatives by law are supposed to return patronage to their members. Since 1990, $15 billion has been repatriated, a satisfying number perhaps, but one that invites a level of derision. Tennessee Congressman Jim Cooper, however, took exception in a 52-page Harvard Journal on Legislation entitled, *Electric Cooperatives: From New Deal to Bad Deal*. In 2008, that tome prompted House Commerce and Energy Chair Henry Waxman to hold a hearing over equity held by electric cooperatives among other grievousness aired in the Harvard study.

Cooper, a Tennessee Congressman representing parts of Nashville and Chattanooga, charged that co-ops held more than $30 billion in equity that rightfully belonged to co-op members who were never told about their accumulated equity which was estimated to be an average of $1,625 per member in 2008. Cooper said co-ops could dramatically reduce rates if they'd merged and, with over 850 electric cooperatives, there were plenty of opportunities. Perhaps most damaging was Cooper's allegations that were true, as it turned out, of financial improprieties of large co-ops like Pedernales Electric located in Johnson City, Texas which was also LBJ's co-op. Pedernales CEO Bernie Fuelberg earned in excess of $1 million in salary and benefits and some members of the co-op's Board of Directors were earning in excess of $100,000 annually—a bit more than the average of $15,000 for many other co-ops. The Pedernales co-op and others booked rooms at the Ritz Carlton and paid for Celine Dion tickets. Another Texas co-op, CoServe, borrowed $1 billion to purchase a golf course, a Westin Hotel, and a shopping center only to declare bankruptcy.[3]

Cooperative largesse, or excess, has occasionally tarnished the rural electric program. The South Carolina-based Tri-County Electric, with rates approaching what FDR saw in the mid-1920s in Warm Springs, saw their board representing 13,600 members holding some fifty meetings at $450 each and netting on average nearly $50,000 annually per director, a position many thought was voluntary.[4] To that total, NRECA offers health insurance to some 100,000 co-op employees which would also include some co-op boards of directors. Given the average age of co-op directors of over sixty, that health benefit is especially expensive. The outlay may have led the Louisiana PUC to declare:

"Regulators and the electric cooperatives that serve about 900,000 Louisiana customers are nearing a deal that would make the most sweeping changes since the 1940s in the way the rural utilities operate. Both sides are agreeing on term limits for board members and how much they'll be reimbursed for attending meetings. But some co-op board members are wanting to keep their health insurance, which was one of the perks that prompted the five elected members of the Public Service Commission to recommend restrictions."[5]

A Louisiana court would later overturn that PUC dictate.[6]

Each year co-ops hold annual meetings allowing members to vote on their board of directors. Not all do so. An Alabama co-op called Black Warrior didn't hold an annual meeting in fifty years which presumably favored the incumbents.[7] According to the Institute for Local Reliance, 72 percent of co-ops see less than 10 percent of their total membership voting for their boards.[8] To be fair, many electric co-ops allow voting by mail or electronically. Some still don't and augue, like some states, that showing up is a requirement for voting.

NRECA has long paid attention to governance. Most co-op directors have obtained their cooperative director certificates which include a course entitled Director Duties and Liabilities. To that, co-op attorneys school directors on appropriate governance behavior which is supplemented by their statewides. If there was any confusion about a director's role, CFC's *Commitment to Excellence: A Guide to Developing Board Policies for Financial Best Practices*[9] would disabuse directors of self-aggrandizement. Here's a succinct summary:

"Electric co-op board duties include loyalty to the membership above self, obedience to laws and bylaws, and duty to care defined as asking pertinent questions and seeking relevant information."

Shannon Clark, CEO of the Wisconsin-based Richland Electric and the past Board Chair of the National Rural Telecommunications Cooperative, defines those duties: "A good director makes the co-op mission as their motivation without regard for self." Clark, who received the Wisconsin Statewide highest service honor, added that directors also need to be both passionate and engaged and to view themselves as servants and ambassadors for the co-ops.

Lake Country Electric Co-op Director and Great River Energy Generation and Transmission Cooperative Board Chair, Bob Bruckbauer, has a feel for governance that is reflective of the Iron Range of Minnesota, the second largest service area in the nation that co-ops serve. The retired school principal says governance is to set policy and work alongside the CEO. Governance means we are responsible for setting policy and the direction of a co-op and avoiding getting into areas that we shouldn't.

So, what is appropriate board compensation?

Connexus Energy, Minnesota's largest co-op, likely pays among the highest per diems nationally at $45,000. Longtime Board Chair Peter Wojciechowski said Connexus consulted with a major accounting firm which suggested per diems should be on an assessment of 1.3 cents per meter per month. Over at Lake Country, Bruckbauer said directors keep a time sheet to track co-op related business. That averages out to $22 an hour, an amount one district meeting attendee observed wouldn't be worth his time. Perhaps the best compensation policy is the one adopted by Federated Rural Electric. That Minnesota co-op, according to CEO Scott Reimer, provides the co-op's nominating committee with the NRECA annual director compensation as well as one that is completed locally for their consideration. The committee decides on the appropriate board compensation. Attendees at the co-op annual meeting then approve that amount.

Excess compensation attracts adverse attention. Increasingly, so does how conspicuous a co-op is.

John Farrell directs the Energy Democracy Initiative at the Institute for Local Self-Reliance. ILSF has taken an avid interest in co-ops which includes listing a scorecard on how well Minnesota co-ops do in nine areas such as listing their board minutes, how to contact board members, their energy resource mix, how to run for the co-op board, the bylaws, and others. That site, known as the MN Local Energy Project, has cousins showing similar scorecards in Kentucky, Georgia, and Montana. Another online co-op watchdog entitled We Own It and described as "pro-co-op, pro-member, pro-democracy" is designed to make electric cooperatives more accountable to their members including citing that nearly 75 percent of all co-ops see less than 10 percent of their membership voting on bylaws and director elections.[10]

Farrell endorsed the co-op model but observed that co-ops need to be far more transparent which he defined as meeting members on their terms and their turf. Farrell said co-ops must strive to ensure members clearly understand how and where their power is generated, how they can affect co-op policy, and how they can run for the board of directors.

The magazine, Fast Company, published an article in 2016 entitled, Why it's so hard to change a bad first impression.[11] The authors concluded that "the news isn't good for anyone who is trying to improve perceptions." Or think about this: At the Oregon Rural Electric Cooperative Association Director Education Conference, NRECA Assistant General Counsel Jessica Healy cited the front-page effect as how would board decisions look like above the crease on page one of the local paper? Or that 60 percent of all Americans, likely including you, are on Facebook which records likes and dislikes as is true with Yelp. Again, it's nearly impossible to change a bad first impression which inevitably leads to consequences.

In the 1990s, co-ops were gripped with proposals allowing customers to choose their electric provider. Known as customer choice, a lobby group called Citizens for a Sound Economy promoted that trend and claimed industry competition would reduce electric bills as high as 43 percent.[12] Enron, once the nation's sixth largest corporation, aggressively promoted customer choice under the Energy Policy Act of 1992 that allowed states to invite competition. Enron manipulated that market and caused rolling blackouts in California which largely ended customer choice programs until CCA arrived.

Community Choice Aggregators, or CCA, is in the words of the Portland, Oregon Willamette Week an electric co-op buyers' club.[13] The big difference between CCAs and other public utilities is that, unlike public utilities, CCAs don't own power plants, poles, or wires—or even do billing. They just buy electricity. The key to the surge in CCAs over the past few years in California is the rise of merchant developers: companies that build large wind and solar plants hoping to sell their power at a profit. Such companies have injected a new level of competition and choice into the utility industry. And that's precisely the caution the 21st Century Report observed, that "If the cooperatives cannot meet the challenges of the new energy marketplace, third parties could move in to fill the void."[14]

If your local business shows a disinterest in your needs, you move on. If an electric cooperative board of directors majors in arrogance and adhering to antiquated energy models that are counter to 89 percent of electric customers who prefer renewable energy, or any number of things that aren't to a customer's liking, then there are any number of options to switch providers, CCA being just one.

Again, we cited that fully half of the Fortune 500 companies that dominated in the 1970s no longer exist. Electric co-ops are approaching ninety years, longer than most because and only because co-ops responded to what their members needed. Those co-op member-owners, with the emphasis on owners, need us more than ever. Co-ops now offer an array of renewable energy, solar solutions, and electric vehicle rates. Co-ops through REDLG have created or retained some 100,000 jobs. All those laudable efforts, however, will be brushed aside if boards disregard what their members are telling them.

See what the We Own It website has to say. Take a look at the different groups like the MN Local Energy Project[15] checklist to see how your co-op compares. Ask, as John Farrell does, whether or not you are reaching your membership wherever they may be.

That is the electric co-op calling. If you choose to ignore that mission, others are already stepping forward to fill in.

Which brings us to the frailty that each electric cooperative must contend with.

Chapter 5

Governance Comeuppance

I n 2018, Randall Thomas, Harwell Wells, and Debra Jeter wrote an article for the Alabama Law Review entitled, Rural Electric Cooperatives and the Surprising Persistence of the Separation of Ownership and Control.[1] Here is some of their thinking:

> "In this Article,[2] we examine a significant and almost completely over-looked business form, the Rural Electric Cooperative (REC). RECs were founded in a moment of optimism during the New Deal. As with other cooperatives, their organizational rules differed sharply from those of for-profit corporations. They were owned by their customers, with each customer-member having one vote irrespective of their energy consumption, and it was hoped these owners would provide active oversight of the REC's managers and activities.[3] Reality has proven otherwise. Corporate governance innovations of the last forty years have passed RECs by, leaving an organizational sector mired in governance dysfunctions stemming from the separation of ownership and control."

The ensuing pages include governance concerns that REA had shortly after Morris Cooke's 12 Minutes of optimism. The authors cited REA's worries[4] about self-dealing, so much so that the model bylaws proposed by REA in the late 1930s, and largely adopted then by the nation's co-ops, proposed banning employment of directors or their relatives and prohibiting directors as candidates for public office or being otherwise employed by IOUs or stores peddling electric appliances.

The early framers were right to be concerned. In the early 1990s, the then Northern Electric Cooperative Association based in Virginia, Minnesota attempted to sell out to Minnesota Power. The board chair of the co-op was a retired Minnesota Power executive. In a presentation in the 1980s to then Nebraska Congresswoman Virginia Smith, Nebraska Rural Electric Association Manager Rex Carpenter was explaining why electricity was still a bargain despite recent rate increases due to new power plant additions. Up jumped a director from the McCook Public Power District, waving a rate card and arguing that propane, which employed him, was far cheaper

Other model bylaw sentiments, still prevalent today, required at least 10 percent[5] of the membership without board approval to merge a co-op or sell to an IOU. Sellout votes now require a much higher threshold. Concerned about proxy voting, the process where members could allow others to vote their interest, the suggested REA bylaws proposed only three proxy votes. Notably, that REA proposal was done to rein in efforts by management to control votes and thus potential bylaw changes by uniformed members.

Perhaps the most notable proposal, particularly for that time, was REA's suggestion that every co-op board include a woman.[6] Early photos show some evidence of that but, for many co-op boards, not only is the absence of a woman jarring, so, too, is the age of directors with many of them resembling Uncle Junior Soprano. In fact, during the 1980s, there were no women directors on any of the Nebraska PPD or co-op boards despite the demonstrable fact that in most families it is the wife who makes many of the spending decisions.

Let's focus upon the three authors' opinion that "Corporate governance innovations of the last forty years have passed RECs by, leaving an organizational sector mired in governance dysfunctions stemming from the separation of ownership and control" and examine a large investor-owned utility.

A $60 million dollar bribe was paid to the Ohio Speaker of the House Larry Householder by FirstEnergy Nuclear Solutions to assist that company by passing a nuclear bailout bill that added 85 cents per month to homeowner bills and raised $150 million to bail out the company's two nuclear plants.[7] That bill has since been suspended. It is difficult to believe that FirstEnergy Nuclear Solutions' board was unaware of that kickover. If they were not, it was an enormous failure to live up to the company's business ethics which company CEO Charles Jones noted: "At FirstEnergy, we are all responsible for upholding high standards and being aware of ethical issues that we may face on the job".[8]

Consider, again, that in the last fifty years fully half of the Fortune 500 companies have gone bankrupt. Creative disruption was a term popularized by Clayton Christensen. He wrote a book with co-author Joseph Bower, *The Innovator's Dilemma,* a book about disruptive technologies and disruptive innovations, and he was responsible for relegating companies to a whatever happened category.[9] Most recently, Sears, an upstart business at least at its inception in 1880, declared bankruptcy. Among the Sears board of directors was Steve Mnuchin, Trump's Secretary of the Treasury.[10] Isn't creative governance intended to address industry products and practices?

Or consider General Electric, whose equipment still generates more than about one-third of the world's electric power according to *Lights Out, Pride, Delusion and the Fall of General Electric* by Thomas Gryta and Ted Mann.[11] GE is the company founded by Thomas Edison and J. P. Morgan. Who can't recall GE's tagline, "We bring good things to life," and that motto was valued at $30 billion. At its peak in 2000, GE was the most valuable company in America and worth almost $600 billion. It had business lines that sprawled across boundaries to touch vast swaths of life in the developed world. GE also featured GE Capital, long an AAA- rated lending agency which at one time was the seventh largest bank in the country according to a June 9, 2005 Wall Street Journal analysis.[12]

The GE board was governed by CEOs of some of the nation's largest investment funds, corporations, and telecommunication companies among other well-known industries and the board was designed to guide GE. General Electric was also a long mainstay of the thirty-company Dow Jones Industrial Average that was part of the answer investors asked daily as to what happened on the Dow. For years, the board counted eighteen directors who earned, on average, $300,000 annually plus the opportunity to take home up to $30,000 worth of GE products over a three-year period.[13]

Jack Welch was the General Electric CEO whose 2001 book, *Straight from the Gut,* was endorsed by Warren Buffet. Welch was so dominant when he was the CEO that it was said the board of directors' responsibility was to applaud him.[14]. His successor, Jeff Immelt, admitted that the board was only "peripherally involved during the various crises that confronted the company." The board did not know that Immelt on his frequent flights nationally and internationally not only took GE's private 737—a board requirement—but a second jet followed in case the 737 carrying Immelt had engine trouble.[15] Here's what The Wall Street Journal said about the GE board that saw the company flounder:

> "But there was plenty of blame to go around. Perhaps most of it should be placed on the board of directors, the independent group that oversees the CEO. Board members claimed to have been unaware of problems and to have gotten bad guidance from external advisers and they said they didn't understand how the company went from good to bad seemingly overnight. Some directors had no experience in GE's business lines, others had trouble staying awake during meetings, and many stumbled away from GE's collapse wondering, 'How could we have known?' It had been their job to know, however, and their job to ask the hard questions that weren't fully answered or were never asked at all. It was their job to oversee management, and it was their job to protect investors from fatal hubris."[16]

We can't help but cite one other example: Theranos. That was a company founded by a Stanford dropout by the name of Elizabeth Holmes. According to the book, *Bad Blood, Secrets and Lies of a Silicon Valley Start-up* by John Carreyou,[17] Theranos at one time was valued at $9 billion based on a technology touted to test for 100 potential diseases from one pinprick of blood. So entranced with that possibility, both Safeway grocery store and Walgreens spent considerable funds to accommodate a testing station that would provide any analysis within minutes. Investors, in particular, were swayed by the Theranos board which included former Secretary of State George Schultz, former US Senate Majority leader and physician Bill First, James Mattis, Trump's first Secretary of Defense, and Betsy DeVos, Trump's Education Secretary. Holmes now faces fraud charges for defrauding investors which, if convicted, could carry a sentence of twenty years.

Keep in mind that those directors were handpicked by the CEO for their financial and strategic acumen. Which perhaps explains why both NRECA and CFC have spent considerable time and effort on governance including the duo's most notable collaboration in 2017 entitled, Electric Cooperative Governance Task Force, covering nearly seventy pages.[18] It really is an outstanding piece of work that the twenty-person task force undertook including defining good governance which the task force said "means having the policies, practices, and culture to facilitate: 1) member engagement in, and democratic member control of, the cooperative; 2) fiduciary oversight of the cooperative's operations and structure; 3) achieving the cooperative's vision, mission, and goals; and 4) acting with integrity, transparency, accountability, and courage.

Let's see how everything stacks up. Historically, criticism of co-ops largely centered on loan programs. Let's return to the Cooper Harvard report and subsequent House Energy and Commerce Committee hearing in June of 2008 which hit co-ops for not returning capital credits. As of January 2017, the NRECA reported that RECs have $55 billion in equity which works out to an average of $2,894 per customer-member. Co-ops were accused of refusing to merge to achieve economies of scale, failure to hold annual meetings, adherence to coal-based generation, and—perhaps the most damaging—financial improprieties of some electric cooperatives for excess compensation, lavish dinners, coveted concert tickets, and other excess.

For a program that provided service to largely rural America where income, longevity, employment, and educational achievement lagged well behind urban areas, it did not do as suggested by Vern Dosch, the CEO of the National Information Solutions Cooperative, whose book, *Wired Differently,* contained compelling advice to "do the right thing, always."[19]

Even before the 2018 report, NRECA had long paid attention to governance. Most co-op directors have obtained their cooperative director certificates which include a course entitled, Director Duties and Liabilities. In addition, co-op attorneys instruct directors on appropriate governance behavior which is supplemented by their statewides. If there was any confusion about a director's role, CFC 's Commitment to Excellence: A Guide to Developing Board Policies for Financial Best Practices would disabuse directors of self-aggrandizement.[20] Here's a succinct summary: "Electric co-op board duties include loyalty to the membership above self, obedience to laws and bylaws and duty to care defined as asking pertinent questions and seeking relevant information."

The 2018 NRECA Electric Cooperative Governance Task Force [21] suggests that "The Task Force supports an electric cooperative being transparent regarding director compensation—beyond simply filing Form 990. For example, the Task Force supports an electric cooperative posting director compensation on its website, reporting director compensation in its annual report or during its annual member meeting, and/or posting its Form 990 on its website."

One issue the Electric Cooperative Governance Task Force chose not to address is the age of directors. It was said by some that I was foolish to invite the CEO of Medtronic, best known as the manufacturer of pacemakers, to a Minnesota Statewide meeting. The then CEO, Bill North, author of the management book entitled, *True North*,[22] was asked to discuss governance, particularly when directors should retire. North cited, of course, the wisdom that age theoretically provides but then advised that at seventy directors should strongly consider stepping down, an opinion not widely shared by those at or approaching that age.

The average age of co-op directors is sixty-two which, according to an April 2019 Diligent Insight, is similar to the Standard and Poor's 500 largest corporation boards age.[23] In 2018, the average age of House Members was fifty-eight and that of US Senators was sixty-two, putting co-op board members in similar age parity. Earlier, it was proffered that boards should reflect their co-op constituency. If age is a consideration, and it should be, then co-ops' board dotage on average is still less than the US Census average of seventy-three years for most rural counties which, of course, is mostly the co-op service area heartbeat. Still, the lengthening of years lessens most everyone's abilities. Here's what the Task Force had to say about that:

> "The Task Force supports an electric cooperative addressing a director who may be legally competent, but appears to lack the physical, mental, or emotional ability to serve as a director competently. Many times, these individuals have served as a director for many years, and served effectively, competently, and well. They often have strong emotional ties to the cooperative and with other directors. Often, they do not recognize or appreciate the degree to which their ability to serve has diminished.

Addressing these directors can be sensitive and difficult. If the director's diminished ability is caused by a disability, then the cooperative should provide any legally required reasonable accommodation. Beyond any legal requirements, however, the Task Force supports an electric cooperative board of directors addressing whether these directors comply with the cooperative's director qualifications and whether they lack the physical, mental, or emotional ability to serve competently. For legal and other reasons, however, the Task Force opposes a director qualification based upon age.

When addressing the director's ability to serve competently, the board presiding officer could speak privately with the director or, perhaps more importantly, with the director's family. The officer could carefully suggest the director resign or not seek re-election. If needed, the board could ask the cooperative attorney to discuss with the director or family whether the director can fulfill his or her fiduciary duty to the cooperative, and note the potential liability associated with breaching the duty. As appropriate, the board presiding officer or attorney could note the possibility of calling a special member meeting to address the director's ability to serve competently."[24]

In addition to that, co-ops might consider a bylaw provision allowing removal of non-performing directors. The National Rural Telecommunications Cooperative includes in their bylaws a two-thirds super majority removal process for cause.

Absent board intervention, a membership will occasionally step in. In 2005, perhaps 2006, members of the Minnesota-based Lake Region Electric Cooperative seized, oddly enough, on the perception that the co-op didn't have sufficient equity. CFC has long advocated 40 percent and that meets financial benchmarks. That percentage may also prevent IOUs from seizing co-ops with much higher equity which would facilitate takeover efforts. While Lake Region hovered in that vicinity, some directors, showing their senility, would complain with their pals about a CEO salary, director misbehavior, and other assorted but perceived wrongdoings while strolling through a McDonald's value menu. Such behaviors should have been addressed by the board and when there was only one, perhaps two, spokespeople for the co-op. That chitchat saw eight of the nine board members voted out of office during the next three elections along with the hiring of a new CEO, Tim Thompson, whose attention to governance issues, if not equity levels, restored the usual noncompetitive board races.

Inept directors, along with excessive compensation, will eventually attract adverse attention. Increasingly, so does representation and so it should.

In May 2016, an organization called Labor Neighbor Research and Training Center and ACORN International released a report called, The Crisis in Rural Electric Cooperatives in the South. The group reported that board members representing southern co-ops (Arkansas, Florida, Kentucky, Louisiana, Mississippi, Tennessee, Alabama, Georgia, North Carolina, South Carolina, Texas and Virginia) were 95.3 percent white and 4.4 percent black. To provide perspective, the co-ops in the states surveyed showed that African American and Hispanic populations were one-third of the total. Texas, whose Hispanic population is not far from 40 percent, counts five Hispanic board members among that state's seventy-three electric cooperatives. Mississippi and Tennessee, which include a sizable African American population, had one Black director.[25] That was in 2012, so, perhaps the numbers have righted themselves but likely not. Likely not, because REA in the mid-1930s anticipated that boards might be self-perpetuating as evidenced by the following citation:

> "Along with encouraging member activism, the REA also tried to block the ability of small groups to gain power over cooperatives. The election of women to boards, along with the Model Act's provision concerning a cooperative's board of trustees, was a clear attempt to diversify a board's membership. While the Model Act required a board to have at least five members, the cooperative's bylaws could set a larger number which the Model Act's Comment explained was included to prevent "undue control by small groups, particularly by boards of trustees."[26]

Think about REA's prescient warning in the 1930s that co-op boards, or trustees, would be monolithic. That has turned out to be the case after nearly ninety years of denying minorities a seat at the co-op table. Do we call that racism? Perhaps we do, or don't, but what we do know is that the historic exclusion of member representation includes people of color and is now systemic. Not only that, an examination of the co-op employees who are minorities is likely similar to minority representation on co-op boards. How many African American co-op CEOs are there? One. That would be Curtis Wynn, CEO of the North Carolina-based Roanoke Electric Cooperative, who also ascended to be chairman of the NRECA board.

There was a time when RUS conducted a civil rights audit of co-ops or, in the case of Nebraska, its public power district. On December 21, 2001 RUS Administrator Hilda Legg issued a bulletin suspending that review which, in retrospect, meant very little. Now it means nothing.[27] But it's anything but nothing to disenfranchised members. Shameful is a quick sentiment but far more important is the disservice a co-op does for its members. Consider the minority-owned businesses that co-ops could attract by offering REDLG funding which would create what every co-op wants: load. To be fair, USDA reports about 11.5 percent of REDLG funding goes to minority-owned businesses.[28] Omitting a sizable population, however, from representation on a co-op board limits, and severely at that, the broad perspectives needed to make smart decisions. All white guys around the table will likely think alike, important perhaps for deciding the board's lunch menu, but not what's important to the membership as a whole. It is not about affirmative action. Membership representation is solely about reflecting the needs of the entire membership which, mostly decidedly, cannot and should not be the province of one skin color.

The book, *Geography of Genius*,[29] said that the most creative places are populated by a diverse population. The best decisions on Who Wants to be a Millionaire came from a diverse audience of all colors and sexual preferences. Eliminating that portion of the population on a co-op board, including women, doesn't necessarily make for an inept board of directors. What it does is limit the board and, subsequently, the co-op's perspective and opportunities which is incredibly shortsighted.

Russell Reynolds Associates, a leading global executive search and assessment firm with more than 300 consultants based in thirty-nine offices worldwide, made this observation:[30]

- A wide range of perspectives, not merely token representation, is critical to effective corporate governance.
- The trend toward diversity is essential as boards look to navigate the complex and dynamic issues that companies now face.
- Boards become greater advocates for diversity as they have more direct beneficial experiences with it.
- It is incumbent upon board members and the candidates themselves to reach out to each other at a time when the adage of "who you know" is being replaced by "how you know them."

If that's not compelling, then states—starting, of course, with California—are mandating that corporate boards include women. With the zeal of We Own It and the Institute for Local Self Reliance, along with any number of groups and none perhaps more important than Black Lives Matter, attention has already been turned to co-op board diversity. Might it not be a good, if not great idea, to ensure your co-op board reflects the membership? If not, then the blame for exclusion will rightly fall on boards of directors, if not the membership which likewise hasn't been sufficiently diligent. An Alabama Law Review article made this observation:

> "The REA also tried exhortation. In 1939 it issued A Guide for Members of REA Cooperatives written in straightforward language and intended to teach members about the cooperative's role as a democratic institution and their role within it. While 'cooperation splendidly demonstrates the adaptability of old-fashioned democracy to new-fashioned problems,' the brochure stated that cooperatives' success requires the 'constant, active participation of a well-informed and loyal membership.' Cooperatives failed when members did not participate. Perhaps they picked a poor board of directors that hired an incompetent manager. Perhaps they allowed a small group of people to control and run the business as they pleased and to feather their own nests."[31]

Evidence suggests that the problem of apathetic membership and board malfeasance was never solved. In the 1950s, REA staffers reported that "the old problems of autocratic and self-perpetuating boards of directors" had reappeared in several states while also complaining that "in far too many of our co-op borrowers, member apathy appears to be still rather widespread." A decade later, Jerry Voorhis, Executive Director of the Co-operative League, writing in support of RECs, nonetheless admitted that while most "electrical cooperatives are strong organizations with loyal, proud memberships," there were cooperatives where "the manager has worked himself into the position of a virtual dictator" and others where members "take electric service as a matter of course."[32]

While there are governance reports and task force exhortations provided by NRECA, CFC, and various statewides, even more compelling should be that those organizations instruct on the necessity of board diversity, providing co-op jobs for the talent the disenfranchised represent, and providing cultivation of skills that they also possess.

There is no greater calling for the twenty-first century electric cooperative than to do so.

Chapter 6

What's in a Name?

Howell Cobb was the fortieth Governor of Georgia from 1851 to 1853. Cobb was also President James Buchanan's Secretary of the Treasury from 1857 to 1860. Cobb, however, is probably best known as one of the founders of the Confederacy, having served as the President of the Provisional Congress of the Confederate States.[1]

Portraits of every Speaker of the US House has adorned the walls of Congress, including Howell Cobb who was the Speaker from 1849 to 1851. Speaker Nancy Pelosi removed Howell Cobb and three other Speakers who were once involved in the Confederacy. Here's what Pelosi said on the Juneteenth (so named for the end of slavery) of 2020 as reported by Politico:[2]

> "'As I have said before, the halls of Congress are the very heart of our democracy,' Pelosi wrote in a letter requesting the removal. 'There is no room in the hallowed halls of Congress or in any place of honor for memorializing men who embody the violent bigotry and grotesque racism of the Confederacy.'"

Cobb County, where Cobb Electric Membership Cooperative claimed its name, isn't named for Howell Cobb. Instead, that county of some 760,000 residents is named for Howell Cobb's cousin, Judge Thomas Willis Cobb, who served as a US Senator, state representative, and superior court judge.[3] Cobb county was one of nine Georgia counties carved out of the disputed territory of the Cherokee Nation in 1832.

Cobb Electric Membership Corporation is named for the county it principally serves, along with portions of three suburban counties directly north of the City of Atlanta—Cobb, Cherokee, and Paulding. All told, Cobb EMC counts more than 200,000 members. Cobb Electric EMC was once called Cobb Energy. The former CEO of Cobb EMC, Dwight Brown, and his board set up Cobb Energy as the for-profit subsidiary of Cobb EMC. The largest stockholders were Dwight Brown and his wife. Cobb Energy charged the EMC a fee on the combined weekly salaries and fringe benefits of the employees, which was initially 2 percent but was later increased to 6 percent and then 11 percent according to court documents.

Truly, that is an incredible story. Let's draw on the report filed by the Marietta Daily Journal on June 20, 2015:[4]

- The forensic audit called Brown a "bully, not a leader" who seldom changed his investments, no matter how inadvisable they were.
- Brown and his wife Mary Ellen collected some $21.3 million from 1996 to 2011.
- Brown controlled the Cobb EMC board by "ensuring they were well compensated and received extraordinary health insurance and retirement payments after leaving the board."
- The EMC board "voted to create Cobb Energy without a business plan or any projects supporting even minimal due diligence."
- After setting up the EMC spin-off, Cobb Energy, Brown created and/or acquired ten other businesses as subsidiaries of Cobb Energy including a mortgage company, a construction company, and even a pest-control service. The auditors found no evidence that Cobb Energy reviewed or approved any business plan for any of those businesses, nor that the board ever discussed such companies' financials or personnel compensation.
- "With one or possibly two exceptions, all of the Cobb Energy spin-offs lost money, some on a grand scale," the auditors wrote. Witnesses told the auditors they had told Brown of the financial drain on multiple occasions but each time were rebuffed.
- Brown also negotiated a long-term $14.7 million lease for the Pataula EMC's facilities in South Georgia in 2005 on a handshake basis with no prior study, which then was approved without question by the then EMC board.

- "Ultimately, due to Cobb Energy's failure to timely remit the electric customer receipts, Cobb EMC was forced to rely on its lines of credit. By 2008, it was near its $125 million credit limit due to the constant drain from Cobb Energy."

The ensuing lawsuits rightfully included the co-op's trustees. Here's the rejoinder Judge Schuster directed at the Cobb Energy Board according to the Marietta Daily Journal of August 15, 2011:[5]

- "Schuster's frustration with the EMC was perhaps most apparent when he, in effect, ridiculed them for supposedly conducting a two-year search to find a replacement for Brown and then trying to rehire him immediately after his retirement with the explanation that they had been unable to find anyone more qualified.
- "Further evidence that Schuster didn't trust the ten directors came when he ordered them to tell him right away what Brown made since he supposedly retired per the court order on Feb. 28. In short, Schuster let it be known to the directors that he didn't want any more weasel words or runarounds from EMC lawyers or PR spin doctors."
- "Finally, before dismissing the embarrassed and humiliated directors, Schuster told them if they had been looking after EMC business and not Brown's, they would have put him on leave of absence after he was indicted instead of continuing to pay him and providing him office space at the EMC headquarters."
- Observers said it was "the tongue-lashing of all tongue-lashings" and suggested that self-respecting directors would have tucked tail and resigned immediately afterward. But that hasn't happened. And in fact, all ten plan to seek re-election!

Here's the final quote from that MDJ article, an observation that every co-op board confuses self-aggrandizement with what's best for the member-owners:

"Chalk it all up as further evidence of the truth of what Dr. Paul Lapides, director of Kennesaw State University's Corporate Governance Center, said about the board in June after its dubious attempt to rehire Brown was vetoed by Schuster, "If there were awards for the worst boards in America, they would make the Top Ten."

There is, of course, a bit more. And that has to do with capital credits. This from the Marietta Daily Journal:[6]

"Members of the Cobb Electric Membership Corp., a nonprofit co-operative, won a proposed settlement of a class action lawsuit that means $98 million will be paid to about 900,000 current and former customers, also called members, including individuals and businesses for their long, long overdue shares of EMC profits, or capital credits, going back to the co-op's formation in 1938."

Among the expenditures Dwight Brown made in 2007 was an upfront payment of $12.7 million to gain the naming rights for a $145 million arena which seats 2750. The arena's name is Cobb Energy Performing Arts Centre. The following is from the December 12, 2017 Marietta Daily Journal which is the basis for all of this information:

"Executives and members of Cobb EMC believe it's high time the Cobb Energy Performing Arts Centre changed its name. That label, many say, is an embarrassing reminder of a long-running controversy that saw the Cobb Energy Management Corporation closed by court order. Trouble is, the Performing Arts Centre's board is not interested in changing the theater's name, saying it has too much brand recognition, and besides, most people don't associate it with the now shuttered company. Proponents of a name change campaign for two reasons: The shame associated with Cobb Energy's tainted history and the hope that Cobb EMC would receive a portion of the revenue from a new naming rights agreement."

Here's an idea Cobb EMC should consider: change its name. Cobb Electric is not named for the leader of the confederacy. Still, Thomas Willis Cobb, a cousin of Howell Cobb, the now deposed House Speaker, at least portrait-wise, was in all likelihood a Confederate sympathizer. If Cobb EMC wants to remove the Cobb Energy name from the performing arts center because it is associated with the disgraceful tenure of Dwight Brown who, it should be noted, saw all his charges dismissed, they should take the next step. That step is to rename Cobb EMC for Henry Aaron, the Atlanta Braves most notable star who, while slugging to break Babe Ruth's 714 homers back in 1974, saw a deluge of hate mail. That loathing reappeared, unbelievably thirty-six years later, when Aaron told US Today[7] of the death threats and slurs he endured. Here's Aaron's recollection of the more than 900,000 pieces of mail he received:

> "I was forbidden to open mail for two and a half years. I had a secretary that had to open all my mail and when the games were over with, I had to go out of the back of the baseball parks."

Co-ops, already long wed to coal-based generation, are making a hasty departure from that bit of carbon nastiness based both on economics and member sentiment. America's sentiment now is, again, Black Lives Matter, a view electric cooperatives, twenty-first century co-ops, should reflect. Here's what Cobb could be renamed: Hammerin Hank EMC. Or Henry Aaron Electric Cooperative. Or Aaron Electric Cooperative. Or Hank's Homerun Electric Cooperative. Or, to be historically correct, Cherokee Electric, to acknowledge their once purloined territory.

Similarly, co-ops like the Minnesota-based Beltrami Electric which, natch, takes its name from Beltrami County, although the co-op's service area covers six other counties, should consider naming the co-op for the Ojibwe Red Lake Indian Tribe. Cherry-Todd Electric, named for the two counties it serves in Nebraska and South Dakota, is also home for the Rosebud Indian Reservation and should differentiate itself by recognizing that American Indian heritage.

Cobb EMC has distinguished itself by delivering broadband to its members, providing innumerable scholarships, having the fifth lowest rates among Georgia utilities, providing funding for Habitat for Humanity, and scoring solar for interested members—all of which underscore the co-op's commitments to their very large customer base.

The Big Think website wrote,[8] "What's in a name? Everything. That's why Cobb EMC and other co-ops need to rethink their names because, yes, they mean everything."

That's not all. In its history dating from 1938, Cobb EMC has yet to have one African American board member. Here's the African American demographics of the three principal counties located in Cobb EMC's service area:

Cobb—25.2 percent
Cherokee—7.4 percent
Paulding—17.5 percent

Like most co-ops, Cobb EMC voting turnout, despite mail ballots, is about 10 percent of the population. It isn't known whether or not minorities have shown an interest in the co-op board, nor is it known if the current or past boards have attempted to recruit minority board members. Now, that co-op and that board should do everything they can to either recruit an African American board member or make him or her an outside advisor. It is an embarrassment that in the long history of the co-op not a single person of color has been recruited to sit on the co-op board despite serving a sizable African American community.

This is the age of Black Lives Matter. This should no longer be the age of white men, and old ones at that, who predominate on co-op boards of directors. It is a regrettable legacy of electric co-ops that haven't made sufficient efforts to recruit the disenfranchised whose ideas, imagination, and vision would be instrumental to the twenty-first century co-op and whose likely contributions would be an answer to can we do it again.

Chapter 7

What We Should Have Done
on Climate Change

I n 1978, Congress was convinced that America was running out of natural gas and it passed the Power Plant and Industrial Fuel Use Act.[1] That mandated utilities to burn coal to generate electricity and included generation and transmission cooperatives (G&Ts). All told, from 1978 when the Power Plant and Industrial Fuel Use Act passed until its repeal in 1987, the electric industry built some eighty gigawatts of coal-based electricity generation or the equivalent of eighty coal-based power plants.[2] The Rural Utilities Service reports outstanding loans totaling $4.5 billion to G&Ts to build coal-based generation. Subsequently, or perhaps consequently, five G&Ts are listed in the top 100 dirtiest carbon dioxide producing plants.[3] That also underscores the maxim that where you stand depends on where you sit. NRECA did not sit well with carbon emissions caps.

In 1997, the Senate voted unanimously to reject the Kyoto protocol. That unanimity held that the United States should not enter into any international climate agreement that did not include comparable emissions commitments by developing countries or that "would result in serious harm to the economy of the United States.[4] That decision would be countermanded six years later when Arizona Senator John McCain and Connecticut Senator Joe Lieberman introduced a capping carbon emission covering about 85 percent of the economy.[5] Their effort failed but a measure passed in 2007 required the EPA to keep track of how many tons of carbon emissions drifted skyward.

2009 saw the concerted effort to pass a cap-and-trade measure. That bill, known as the Waxman-Markey bill, proposed a cap and trade system under which the government would set a limit or cap on the total amount of greenhouse gases that could be emitted nationally.[6] Companies would then buy or sell, i.e., trade permits to emit those gases which would be primarily carbon dioxide. The cap would be reduced over time to reduce total carbon emissions. The legislation proposed a cap on total emissions over the 2012–2050 period. The measure also provided free allowances for the emission of greenhouse gases. After allowances were initially distributed, entities would be free to buy and sell them which would be the trade part of the program. Those entities that emitted more of that Periodic Table STD faced a higher cost which would provide an economic incentive to reduce emissions. Key elements of the bill included:

- Required electric utilities to meet 20 percent of their electricity demand through renewable energy sources and energy efficiency by 2020.
- Subsidized new clean energy technologies and energy efficiency.
- Protected consumers from energy price increases estimated to cost American families less than a postage stamp per day.
- Set the same target for reductions in other greenhouse gases including methane, derived largely from natural gas extraction.
- Included a renewable electricity standard which largely exempted co-ops except for those sent more than four million MWh through their lines.[7]

The House eventually passed that measure but it did so with notable opposition from NRECA. A New York Times article dated June 19, 2009[8] reported that then NRECA CEO Glenn English expressed the nation's co-op opposition because the measure did not provide adequate carbon credits to the co-ops. Instead, the carbon trading scheme, largely engineered by the Edison Electric Institute or EEI, which is the trade association for investor-owned utilities, gave a larger share to mainly IOUs that had earlier invested in renewable energy. EEI argued that those early investments should be recognized. Of note were northwest co-ops that received a hydro bounty from the Bonneville Power Administration and, to a lesser extent, those getting watered down kW from the Western Area Power Administration. Those co-ops could see up to 100 percent of carbon credits, well beyond what they might need, but which could substantially trade at the expense of Midwest-based co-ops raised on carbon. To their credit, Oregon, Washington, and Idaho didn't raise a fuss and acknowledged that under Waxman-Markey G&Ts on average would see 40 percent less carbon credits than their IOU counterparts. To reiterate, a cap-and-trade system like that envisioned by Waxman and Markey would set an overall ceiling on heat-trapping gases and would force businesses to buy and sell a limited number of allowances representing their emissions.

Once the bill passed the House, Senate Democrats engaged in long talks with the G&Ts on what they wanted. Those conversations included then Massachusetts Senator John Kerry meeting with G&T representatives to see what the measure could accommodate in the way of co-op concerns. Here's what then NRECA Legislative Director Kirk Johnson had to say:

> "I was in the meeting that several G&T CEOs and Glenn English had with Senator Kerry back in the summer of 2009. Senator Kerry asked the group what was most important for the co-ops but no G&T asked for forgiveness of RUS debt at that discussion. Generally, they asked for a set of rules that they could rely upon for the life of the power plants and to not have a continuous drip of new rules and regulations. Largely the conversation focused on certainty so that they could make operational and economic decisions without having to worry about when the next shoe would drop. Senator Kerry made no promises to accommodate co-op concerns but opened a dialogue that obviously went nowhere in the big picture."

English subsequently held a weekly Friday conference call with Statewide CEOs to learn of their concerns and to report on the status of the bill. The consensus was opposition. Which gives rise to the question of what could the co-ops have negotiated?

The co-ops, particularly the G&Ts, should have asked in exchange for phasing out their coal fleet that their accumulated RUS and private lender debt associated to build those plants be forgiven. In exchange, the co-ops would borrow an equivalent amount of that forgiven debt to build or buy renewable energy and provide solar and energy conservation for its members. That never happened. NRECA membership, much enamored with coal that was driven by billions of dollars spent on that lump of energy and mandated by the 1978 Fuel Use Act, simply couldn't ask for change as they were driven by ideology that was reinforced by aligning if not belonging to various pro-coal groups. In addition to all that, co-ops were led by management and boards that were both raised on coal and schooled in the fine arts of responding, "Hell no" to proposals that ran counter to their mindsets.

Generation and Transmission cooperatives could also have used securitization to pay for their coal-based debt. Another way to say securitization is refi, as in I'm gonna refinance my house with a lower interest rate. Here's how that might have worked. Fundamentally, securitization is a financing mechanism through which an independent enterprise is established to 1) issue bonds; 2) sell the bonds to investors; 3) use the proceeds from the bond sales to buy out the utilities' stranded assets, which removes the stranded assets from the utilities' rate bases; and 4) place charges on consumers' electric bills for a limited amount of time to repay the bond investors. Such securitization mechanisms require legislative action at the state level to establish the securitization enterprise and provide the legal authority for it to collect and make payments to the parties involved.

Looking back, a dozen years perhaps could not have seen that the price of solar would drop precipitously. More important, the rise of natural gas reserves discovered in the various states would eventually make G&T coal-based generation uneconomic. That would have been possibly an estimated $8.4 billion hit and one that the IOUs would have opposed if not most Republican members of Congress.

Still, forgiveness of the debt removes that particular carbon liability from the G&T books and, even years later, makes great sense particularly since Kirk Johnson's observation centered on the ever-increasing regulatory noose. Johnson also famously made the observation that co-ops could address their carbon emission burden either through legislation or regulation. Unfortunately, they chose the latter which saw mandated carbon emissions imposed by Obama's EPA making the co-op coal fleet uneconomic, a burden that would later be lifted by the Trump Administration to embrace coal. Elections always sway energy policies. Cap and trade saw the same popularity as did Obamacare, at least at the polls. The 2010 election[9] saw sixty-five House members who voted for the Waxman-Markey bill shuttled off to lobbying jobs or heading up trade associations.

The co-ops asserted for a long time that foregone carbon emissions would cost a bundle. A September 15, 2016 article in The New York Times[10] reported that The Energy Policy Institute at the University of Chicago asked how Americans felt about various issues related to climate and energy and the answers seemed to bear out the opinions of the co-ops. Respondents were asked if they would support a fee on their monthly electricity bill to combat climate change. 43 percent surveyed were unwilling to pay a monthly fee but the intensity of preferences of the other 57 percent also tells of something important. Both camps say something about the political challenges facing adoption of a climate policy.

The Energy Policy Institute poll, however, was undermined by a survey done by the right-leaning Cato Institute in 2019 which reported that 68 percent of households would not pay $10 a month to reduce carbon emissions.[11] If the membership didn't want it, and that's who the co-ops purport to represent, then the co-ops would do everything possible to ensure that they'd hold the line on environmental legislation if not regulation that would exceed what the co-ops thought was the cost-benefit. Which is what was done. But what if there had been the opportunity to take the forgiven bucks to invest into renewable energy. Here's what might have happened:

- In 2020, Morgan Stanley predicted, "Replacing coal with cheaper renewable energy could save electricity customers as much as $8 billion each year."[14]
- Science Daily in October 2019 posited, "For every megawatt of electricity produced using natural gas instead of coal, the water withdrawn from rivers and groundwater drops by 10,500 gallons, and water consumed for cooling and other plant operations and not returned to the environment drops by 260 gallons. Switching to solar or wind power could boost these savings even more."[15]
- Forbes Magazine in January 2020, "It is now cheaper to save the climate than to destroy it. Capacity installation trends reflect this economic reality, with new wind and solar generation coming online at a breakneck pace."[16]

- In 2018, the Rocky Mountain Institute calculated that the Tri-State Generation & Transmission Association (Tri-State) and its member electric cooperatives, through scaled procurement of cost-effective renewable energy projects while maintaining system reliability requirements, could save $600 million through 2030 on a net present-value basis and minimize the risk of rate increases associated with continued reliance on legacy generating assets by 30–60 percent.[17]
- In April of 2020, Bloomberg Green reported, "Solar and onshore wind power are now the cheapest new sources of electricity in at least two-thirds of the world's population, further threatening the two fossil-fuel stalwarts—coal and natural gas. The levelized cost of electricity for onshore wind projects has fallen 9 percent to $44 a megawatt hour since the second half of last year. Solar declined 4 percent to $50 a megawatt hour."[18]

Author Robert Bryce made this observation to the Los Angeles Times in February of 2017: "Just as problematic for the industry's future: to increase wind-energy production to the levels needed to displace significant quantities of coal, oil and natural gas will require erecting more—and taller—turbines (new models reach to 700 feet). But the more turbines that get installed, and the taller they are, the more nearby residents are likely to object. Wind energy simply requires too much territory. That means we can't rely on it for major cuts in emissions. Indeed, the more wind energy encroaches on small towns and suburbs, the more resistance it will face. That resistance will come from homeowners told me, 'We feel this renewable energy push is an attack on rural America.'"[19]

Bryce also submitted that testimony to the US Senate Energy and Natural Resources Committee: "Renewable energy's land-use problem is directly related to the issue of scale. If we are to dramatically increase the use of wind energy, it will require dramatic increases in the amount of land dedicated to that purpose.[20] That was made clear by author Vaclav Smil in his 2010 book, *Energy Myths and Realities: Bringing Science to the Energy Policy Debate*. Smil wrote that relying on wind turbines to supply all US electricity would 'require installing about 1.8 terawatts of new generating capacity,' which he explained, 'would require 900,000 square kilometers of land. For perspective, that's a land area twice the size of the state of California."[21]

Still, wind energy, according to the American Wind Energy Association, continues to grow and they noted, "Wind energy also became the largest source of renewable electricity in the US in 2019, generating over 7 percent of the country's electricity. To put that into perspective, wind now generates enough electricity to meet the demands of California, the world's fourth largest economy, and New Jersey combined. At the state level, wind provided more than 20 percent of the electricity generated in six states: Iowa, Kansas, Maine, North Dakota, Oklahoma, and South Dakota. In Iowa and Kansas, wind is now the single largest source of electricity generation. Both states generated over 40 percent of their electricity from wind power last year.[22]

Which brings us back to what G&T should have told Senator John Kerry, now voiced by these guys:

> According to research by the Center for Rural Affairs, Clean up the River Environment, and We Own It, 53 G&Ts hold $3.4 billion in US Department of Agriculture Rural Electric Service loans and $41.8 billion in loan guarantees, $8.4 billion of which is directly tied to coal infrastructure as of 2010. The federal government and RUS could simply cancel the debt of rural electric cooperatives and rural municipal utilities associated with fossil fuel investments that they hold. This could be tied to specific and strict requirements for a renewable portfolio standard for all participating rural electric cooperatives to achieve 100 percent renewable energy by 2030 and a requirement that the G&Ts and joint action agencies eliminate mandates for high amounts of the co-ops' or municipal utilities' generation to come from long-term power supply contracts.

More telling is how co-ops could have used the $6 billion or so Congress appropriated to RUS to loan to co-ops. The Local Institute for Self Help observed in 2007 that those funds could have been spent this way[24]:

$6 Billion for Rural Energy Efficiency would:

- Save $32 billion in electricity costs for rural electric member-owners over twenty years
- Create 81,000 rural jobs installing energy efficiency improvements
- Provide enough power for 32 million homes for a year
- Cut carbon dioxide emissions by 223 million metric tons

But it's not just for energy efficiency. What if $6 billion was invested in renewable energy like solar power?

$6 Billion for Rural Solar Energy would:

- Install 2,000 megawatts of solar power, seven times more than is in the entire Midwest
- Save $5.3 billion in electricity costs for rural electric member-owners over twenty years
- Create 14,000 rural jobs installing solar power
- Provide enough power for 265,000 homes for a year
- Cut carbon dioxide emissions by 1.8 million metric tons

The cooperatives could also make money offering that program. The USDA allows utilities to re-loan the money to individuals at up to 1.5 percent interest above their own borrowing rate of 3.3 percent. On loans of $6 billion, rural electric utilities would have a margin of $59 million per year re-loaning the money to their members

Politically, could the co-ops have done it? Perhaps. In 2019, the co-ops through NRECA successfully lobbied legislation introduced by Alabama Congresswoman Terri Sewell and Nebraska Representative Adrian Smith. That measure made it clear that storm restoration funds from FEMA and loans and grants to build broadband infrastructure would not count against the 85-15 rule. That particular ratio says co-ops must receive at least 85 percent of their revenue from their members. If non-member revenues exceed 15 percent, the co-op must pay taxes on their margins which, in any event, should have reverted to capital credits. The Sewell-Smith Rural Act made it clear that FEMA assistance and other largesse to expand broadband would be exempt from the 85-15 law. All told, it was a major victory for NRECA and evidence of its standing on Capitol Hill.[25]

Could NRECA do the same to get Congress to forgive RUS loans for coal-based load generation? Presidential candidates, including now Vice President Kamala Harris, suggested that Congress forgive the co-ops' federal coal debt contingent on the G&T and instead that the co-ops should invest in renewables.[26]

Each May, NRECA holds its legislative conference where some 3,000 co-op leaders come to Washington DC to press for legislation important to co-ops. Given the burgeoning efforts to transition to a 100 percent renewable portfolio, already in place in several states and proposed in even more, doing so could enjoy the support of urban legislators like Congresswoman Ocasio-Cortez and Vice President Kamala Harris as well as Members of Congress representing rural areas that have long been supporters of electric cooperatives.

Think not? Then think about the increasing number of states hawking 50–100 percent renewable energy requirements. Then contemplate G&Ts that cover multiple states and the difficulty they will certainly encounter attempting to match up with those differing portfolios, not to mention the increasing regulatory antipathy toward coal. We should have made the case for debt forgiveness based on the 1976 Fuel Use Act in 2009. We should do it now. Except that perhaps we should determine the benefit all this spending is purported to produce.

Chapter 8

New Green Deal
(Why It Might Not Matter)

Even before the New Green Deal was unveiled, Pope Francis in 2015 weighed in with his environmental encyclical.[1] that climate change has grave implications. While critics didn't put a price tag on the Pope's environmental utterance, they did so with the New Green Deal authored by Brooklyn Congresswoman Alexandria Ocasio-Cortez and Massachusetts Senator Ed Markey. In February 2019, the center-right American Action Forum[2] estimated that the plan could cost between $51–$93 trillion over the next decade. They estimated its potential cost at $600,000 per household. Here's what Ocasio-Cortez and Markey envision:[3]

- A low-carbon electricity grid,
- A net zero emissions transportation system,
- Guaranteed jobs,
- Universal health care
- Guaranteed green housing
- Food security

The Senate dismissed that measure on a 57–0 vote which saw most of the Democratic Senators failing to vote.[4] Given the majority of states that have enacted some parts of the New Green Deal, perhaps the overarching measure doesn't matter.

The National Council of State Legislatures,[5] a trade association representing state legislatures, reports that twenty-nine states in addition to Washington, DC and three territories have established renewable portfolio standards (RPS) while eight states and one territory have set voluntary renewable energy goals. Most states' renewable energy targets are between 10 and 45 percent although seven states and Washington, DC have requirements of 50 percent or greater. Some states only require investor-owned utilities (IOUs) to adhere to an RPS while others include electric cooperatives and municipal utilities although requirements are typically equivalent to or lower than those for IOUs.

Southern state legislative bodies have largely ignored renewable energy goals or mandates. Georgia's rural electric co-ops, however, hope to install 1,000 MW of renewable capacity by 2021, a sufficient capacity to serve 180,000 homes. According to a Real Clear Energy report from January 2019, farms and ranches in 2017 received $267 million in wind farm lease payments with much of that derived from the G&Ts serving those rural areas.[6]

Other states, particularly California and ten Eastern states that formed a regional greenhouse gas initiative (RGGI)[7] have developed a cap and trade to reduce carbon emissions. Additional states are looking at a carbon-free environment within thirty years. The eleven states that have carbon emission reduction programs are about 10 percent of the Union:[8]

- Five states have enacted 100 percent carbon free standards representing 11 percent of national electric sales.
- Four more states are leaning toward a 100 percent carbon-free standard that, if adopted, would cover nearly 25 percent of the country's population.
- Nine states have either goals or executive office directives to reduce carbon emissions.
- New York, Minnesota, Illinois, and Colorado are using the social cost of carbon to measure and reduce CO2 impacts for new fossil fuel power plants.
- There is also this financial signal: Morgan Stanley[9] became the first major US bank to set a goal of net-zero financed emissions by 2050, the latest sign that the financial sector aims to tally its contribution to climate change and mitigate the risks it poses to their assets according to a September 29, 2020 Politico article.[10] In the last four years, Morgan Stanley forked over $96 billion. It's competitors, including JPMorgan Chase, Wells Fargo, and Citibank, have all financed more than double that during the same time period.[11]

- In what is scaring off the collective Towncraft britches of Basin Electric members, an effort called Insure Our Future has been successfully urging insurance companies not to cover utilities that own fossil fuel projects. Basin Chief Financial Officer Steve Johnson told a Basin annual meeting, held over Zoom, that "the group has been relatively successful."[12]

The social cost of carbon, also known as externalities, attempts to quantify the economic impact of greenhouse gases on the environment. It's not an exact science as the social cost ranges from $800 per ton to $1 per ton.[13] Minnesota regulators in 2017 raised the cost from 44 cents which had been the benchmark first adopted in 1993. The Minnesota Public Utilities Commission voted to increase that level of 44 cents by nearly a thousand-fold to $43.06 per ton by 2020.[14] Not surprising, the Trump Administration priceed carbon emissions at the $1 menu price.[15]

President Trump called climate change a hoax. While states that supported him, like Texas which derives 20 percent of its energy from wind, and Iowa that clocks in at 36 percent, Trump derides wind generation and believes that it causes cancer. Vermont Senator Bernie Sanders, a leading Presidential candidate before dropping out, promised he would end all fossil fuel generation and the cessation of fracking for natural gas with steep fines for energy producers in addition to providing funding for poorer nations. All told, the Sander's plan would have cost some $17 trillion.[16]

The consulting firm, Wood Mackenzie, noted in Utility Dive in June, 2019 that getting to 100 percent renewables by 2030, a target of Democratic Presidential candidate and Washington Governor Jay Inslee, would cost $4.5 trillion or $35,000 per US household. Wood Mackenzie opined that date simply couldn't be met.[17]

Keep in mind that frack gas has created some 725,000 jobs between 2005 and 2012[18] and has resulted in an 18 percent drop in carbon emissions based on 2019 data.[19] That's the lowest CO_2 output since 1975.[20] While natural gas has 50 percent less carbon emissions than does coal, CO_2 emissions at some point will increase based on the level of natural gas used for generation. In addition to that, leaky natural gas wells produce methane which is twenty-five times more potent than a greenhouse gas which is what coal-based generation produces.[21] Replacing any sort of natural gas with a Sanders mandate of 100 percent renewables by 2030 largely accounts for the incredible price tag.[22]

The plan of former Vice President Biden, now President Biden, was estimated at $2 trillion and embraces many of the renewable energy and carbon emissions goals proposed in the New Green Deal. Biden's proposals include the lofty goal of eliminating carbon emissions from the electric sector by 2035 by, among other things, investing in weatherizing homes and developing a nationwide network of charging stations for electric vehicles. Much of the tab to reach zero by 2035 will be paid by a carbon tax, an idea once floated by President Obama.[23]

The State of Oregon, whose electricity is generated exclusively by either wind, nuclear, and the state's huge allocation of hydroelectricity, ranks forty-seventh in the nation in per capita carbon emissions.[24] Nonetheless, the Democratically controlled Oregon House and Senate have a sufficient edge to deny any Republican opposition to a cap and trade which that body has advocated for several years. Oregon modeled its plan after California's plan where cap-and-trade auctions have raised $12.5 billion in state revenue since 2012 according to the California Air Resources Board. If SB 1530 is enacted, when the program begins in 2022 the Oregon government will initially own allowances and sell them to businesses by holding auctions. The government will also give some allowances away.[25] According to the Oregon Legislative Revenue Office, auction money will go into state funds specified in the bill including those for highways, climate investments, a greenhouse gas initiative, and schools. For example, proceeds from the climate fund would support the State Forestry Department's wildfire mitigation efforts,[26] a pressing need given Oregon's forests along with co-op poles that were torched in the fall of 2020.

Neighboring Washington State likewise has agitated for some type of carbon tax but has seen ballot initiatives purporting to do so failed. Oregon's carbon emission revenue scheme failed on, oddly enough, an attendance requirement. Despite the fact that Democrats hold a wide majority in the thirty-member body, they need at least twenty to conduct business.[27] Twelve GOP state senators who were decidedly opposed to the cap-and-trade measure choose not to attend, some defecting to Idaho to escape the Oregon State Patrol sent to fetch them—twice in 2019 and 2020. Subsequently, the measure failed.

Distributed Energy Resources

In the 1980s, Nebraska's public power districts offered load control to irrigators as a way to manage peak usage of electricity. Reducing the peak meant potentially huge savings for those PPDs and Nebraska co-ops. Nebraska, along with Oregon and Washington, are the only states where public power districts are found. PPDs are political subdivisions similar to co-ops but without the requirements to pay capital credits and hold annual meetings. Directors, however, are largely elected from among the prescribed PPD service area.

The power bill that PPDs paid to their power supplier, in this case the Nebraska Public Power District or Tri-State, was based on the highest number of KW used. Since irrigation is mainly a summertime activity, Nebraska systems, as would be true for every irrigating utility, showed huge spikes in power consumption requiring, at least back in the 1980s, construction of baseload plants to meet that demand. Today, of course, utilities meet peak demand with gas turbine peaking plants but they, too, have become problematic with the EPA issuing hours of service limiting the diesel emissions of many peaking plants. In exchange for load control, the demand charge, or KW charge, was reduced to reflect the savings to the co-op.

There is yet another governance lesson to be learned from and in this case it is irrigation rates. In the 1980s, Wheat Belt PPD located in Sidney, Nebraska implemented a policy that said any new irrigation customers would have to pay a higher demand charge because they were the reprobates that added to the peak at the expense of existing customers. Related or not, the majority of the Wheat Belt board of directors were irrigators. The Court, upon hearing a complaint from the new irrigators, quickly disabused the board of dual rates.[28]

On a similar scale, upper Midwest co-ops allowed for dual fuel heaters to control their peaks which generally occurred in the winter months in order to avoid the necessity of building baseload plants. Co-op members who participated in dual fuel—generally using wood stoves as their alternative—would fire up the stove when the co-op interrupted the flow of electrons. Generally, the dual fuel rate didn't occur that often but, when it did, co-op members were quick to complain and particularly if they weren't around to stoke the embers.

More impressive, perhaps, was early efforts by Great River Energy to store energy in the evening when electric usage diminished. Instead of curtailing loads like air conditioning, GRE and its members sold at a discount or in some cases gave away Marathon water heaters. That generosity allowed GRE members to store wind. Tied to Minnesota's 2007 25 percent renewable energy mandate,[29] GRE along with other utilities added vast amounts of wind generation to their portfolio. Wind resources are generally stronger after Channel 5 News signs off signaling the end of the day and curtailment of the residential electric load. Instead of selling those wind resources into the market generally at a loss, GRE through the genius of Gary Connet, then Director of Demand-Side Management and Member Services, literally created a battery out of more than 80,000 water heaters that were heated at night using low-cost wind resources and played out hot water during peak times.[30] The savings to GRE, its members, and the customers were phenomenal. There was a 40–50 percent reduction in a customer's water heater rate which is one of the higher-cost home units.

We need to go back in time to talk about 1978 PURPA in order to provide a perceptive on distributed energy resources. During the Carter years, the same Administration responsible for the 1976 Fuel Use Act also promoted the Public Utility Resource Policy Act or PURPA.[31] In particular, PURPA 210 required utilities to purchase generating resources produced by their customers at the avoided cost rate. Avoid costs, in that case, meant the wholesale rate the G&T sold to its members, although not necessarily.

According to a January 2020 American Public Power Association news-letter,[32] under PURPA an electric utility's cost to buy power from a QF or qualifying facility is not supposed to exceed what it would have cost the utility to generate the power itself, a concept that FERC refers to as avoided cost. Although the Federal Energy Regulatory Commission or FERC establishes guidelines for calculating avoided costs, PURPA generally gives state public utility commissions the responsibility for determining the avoided costs for the utilities they regulate. The Minnesota PUC, for example, mandated that utilities including electric cooperatives would pay retail rates for any renewable energy project under 40 KW. Subsequently, most projects clocked in at 39.5 KW.

As Danielle Powers of Concentric Power Advisers opined,[33] "Much has changed in the energy landscape since PURPA was established over forty years ago. The generation of electricity is now open to competition in many regions across the country, and wholesale markets provide a vehicle for many of these non-utility power producers to sell their power. Meanwhile, technological advances and renewable policy mandates have driven wholesale power prices to all-time lows. The prices that many QFs are receiving for their energy contracts signed in the past twenty years are well above current market prices."

The value of self-generation first manifested by PURPA, allowed for co-generation up to eighty MW and would not only be supplanted by solar panels but would see a vast new pricing mechanism. In Minnesota, the 2013 legislative session saw legislation requiring all utilities to adopt an energy portfolio that included at least 1.5 percentage solar resources. The co-ops objected saying the cost to do so would be between $800 million and $1 billion based on curtailed generation and the cost of adding solar. Those estimates led to co-ops being exempted, not an unfamiliar strategy. You may recall the cost of solar in 1977 was about $77 a watt. In 2013, the cost had dropped to 77 cents a watt. In 2020, the cost of some panels per watt was 30 cents. What worried co-ops, however, was the consideration of the value of solar. The Minnesota-based Institute for Local Self Reliance in 2014 defied VOS as:[34]

- Avoiding the purchase of energy from other polluting sources
- Avoiding the need to build additional power plant capacity to meet peak energy needs
- Providing energy for decades at a fixed prices
- Reducing wear and tear on the electric grid

Using those definitions produced widely different rates. The solar community back in 2014 said solar should be priced at 16 cents. That was some 60 percent higher than the co-ops' rate to its members. Based on PURPA, it was close to 266 percent more if the average wholesale rate from the G&T was 6 cents. Said another way, if 4 percent of a co-op's customers installed solar at 16 cents and was reimbursed per kWh, the rates to the remaining customers would increase 11 percent. That inequity became a rallying cry that co-op members unable to afford the cost of solar shouldn't be required to pay for those who could.

Then again, co-ops have rewarded their members for aligning their energy usage with that of the co-op. The payback was reduced rates for irrigators and for those acceding to interruptions for air conditioning and heating systems and discounted hot water rates. Why not pay customers for power produced by their solar panels? Well, that has happened.

As of 2016, forty-one states have implemented net metering which requires the utilities to pay for excess watts a customer's solar panels produce beyond what they use.[35] The beyond what they use item is generally a bill credit. Of course, the VOS is based on avoided cost, the avoidance of using the grid, and the catch-all, societal benefits, which is why Xcel Energy says solar based on Minnesota's VOS values is estimated to rise to 25 cents per kWh.

Some states, particularly New York, are now promoting distributed energy resources. That is how Utility Dive describes DER:[36]

"DERs like customer-sited solar, batteries, and electric vehicle chargers hold the promise of revolutionizing the power system, allowing customers to take greater control of their electricity usage and potentially replacing some traditional grid infrastructure. That's a sea change for an industry that for a century faced little competition and relied on massive, customer-financed grid investments to provide electricity.

Utilizing residentially produced power could eliminate the need for new infrastructure or, more likely, could rethink both bulk power systems and the distribution networks which have been in place for close to 100 years. The proposition is that utilities, while distributed energy resources are limited, need to take proactive steps to reconfigure their current wires system to accommodate more rooftop solar and energy storage, the two leading energy resources."

Perhaps it is instructive to recall some history. In her outstanding book entitled *The Grid*, author Gretchen Bakke writes about Sam Insull's efforts to consolidate the various electric providers in Chicago in 1892. When Insull arrived in the then meat packing town, there were eighteen central station electricity providers in the downtown area plus another 500 private power plants, all limited as would be true with DER by voltage.[37] Five years later according to Bakke, "Insull owned all their generating stations, whole hosts of small power plants that were in his opinion not good for much. The era of small power was over."[38] Insull accomplished what he did through the economies of scale represented by large power plants, adding load through reduced pricing, and offering incentive rates as a way to build load factor and increasing the efficiency of power plants which was a practice that would continue for well over a century until climate change and storm-related outages, some lasting weeks, such as was the case in Hurricane Sandy and the increasing popularity of solar.

Solar, likewise, is following the Insull model according to SolarCity, a subsidiary of Tesla. The majority of SolarCity's customers enter into twenty-year contracts with SolarCity to purchase the electricity generated by their solar energy system on an ongoing basis just like they are currently paying their utility bills.[39] SolarCity is unique among solar installers. The company is a fully integrated solar company responsible for everything from production of the solar modules, to sourcing financing, to installation, and to ongoing monitoring.[40]

Even garden solar plants which sell solar panels to acquisitive customers unable or willing to install panels on their roofs, can afford to do so based on economies of scale. Said another way, building a 40 KW solar array is cheaper per kWh than installing a 6 KW system on your roof, a lesson we are still learning from Professor Insull.

The 21st Century Report, for those still keeping count, said,[41] "Consumers will be active participants in deterring their energy needs." That includes more than half of all electric cooperative consumers who now reside in metropolitan counties and, as the report counsels, if they cannot obtain the energy sources they want, "they will get them from third-party providers." Which not only suggested aggressive marketing of subscribing to solar gardens but also training line workers to install solar panels on roofs, as some co-ops are already doing. In addition, co-ops should consider tabulating renewable energy credits that solar and other sources of renewal energy might produce which could fund a carbon-based individual retirement account, a subject in chapter 14.

Chapter 9

The Cost of Climate

The listing of books about climate change has its own Wikipedia page. One prolific author on the page is Bill McKibben who has written over a dozen books. McKibben also writes an occasional column for The New Yorker including one in March 2021[1] where he questioned the need to build more gas stations. McKibben takes particular aim at Costco for planning to build a multi-pump station in California. That state and General Motors plan on going all electric in fourteen years. Gas at Costco on average is 21 cents less than what you'd pay, say, at your local Shell station.

U.S. News and World Report cheerily advises its readers that with the federal tax credit of $7,500—although applicable only to car companies that haven't sold over 165,000 EV—you can score an electric vehicle for under $50,000.[2] Making it available to almost nobody. Then there's state mandates. Minnesota Governor Tim Walz wants to emulate California's zero emission vehicle plan by 2024. That would require Honest Eddie's car lots to feature more EVs than those powered by gasoline. Besides Minnesota and California, ten other states have joined the all-electric queue.

Less than 2 percent of cars bent on the Cannonball Run are electric. And there's an actual group called Coalition Opposing New Gas Stations.[3] Of course, you could point to early solar whose cost per kWh placed it well outside the mainstream price of coal-backed electrons. Today, it's cheaper than almost anything else. Then again, these are cars and the cost of batteries isn't privy to Swanson's Law. Oh, you haven't heard that term? It's the equivalent to Moore's Law which states that the speed and capability of computers increase every couple of years and we will pay less for them. For solar, Swanson's law is the observation that the price of solar tends to drop 20 percent for every doubling of cumulative shipped volume. At present rates, costs go down 75 percent about every ten years.[4]

Here's a perspective. The Waxman-Markey measure that passed the House in 2009 proposed a cap-and-trade system which over time would aim to reduce the amount of carbon dioxide emitted. What's the cost of Waxman-Markey? The difference is staggering and was noted by the 2009 report issued by the Center for Climate and Energy Solutions:

- MIT predicted the bill would cost $3,100 for each household.
- The conservative Heritage Foundation plugged the cost at $4,300 annually.
- By comparison, the American Council for an Energy Efficient Economy said Waxman-Markey would save each household $750 in 2020 and that there was a projected savings of $3,900 a decade later.

The Paris Accord signed in 2015 was endorsed by nearly every country, 197 at last count and including the US after a Trump-imposed hiatus. The Accord proposed to limit global temperature increases to 2°C. Bjorn Lomborg wrote in his book, *False Alarm*, that there has never been an official estimate of the cost to limit warming to 2°C.[5] According to Lomborg, the cost to the world would be $1–2 trillion per year beginning in 2030. The benefit, again in Lomborg's calculation, is less than.05°C. Environmentalists might disagree. The National Resource Defense Council[6] said inaction would cost some $6 trillion in the next decade and a staggering loss of global GDP of 25 percent by 2100. Copping to "we will always have Paris" would produce some $19 trillion in both clean energy and energy efficiency.

A roundup of world leaders in 197 countries who are worried about climate change is impressive. Keep in mind, however, that in 1928 sixty-two countries signed the Kellogg-Briand Pact in which the signatories agreed not to use war to settle disagreements.[7] Three years later, Japan, an original endorser, invaded Manchuria.

Like the Kellogg-Briand Pact, the Paris Accord contains no enforcement mechanism. A 2018 survey found that only 17 of the 157 countries that promised emission cuts in the Paris Agreement have done so. The climate change contributors that have not made emission cuts are the United States, China, India, Russia, Saudi Arabia, and the United Kingdom.

Lomborg cites New Zealand whose Prime Minister Helen Clark vowed in 2007 to be carbon neutral by 2020. Instead, that country's carbon emissions have increased by 137 percent. Its new goal is now 2050.[8] Cutting that particular toxicity by half by 2050 would cost $19 billion annually. That's for a country the size of South Carolina.

Let's turn to Texas. Brazos Electric is that state's oldest G&T and supplies nearly 4,000 MW of the good stuff to sixteen co-ops serving some 1.5 million Lone Star residents. The G&T was first formed in 1941 and later filed for bankruptcy due to a $1.8 billion bill from the Electric Reliability Council of Texas or ERCOT. That takes some explaining if, for no other reason, than to dwell on the near impossibility of arresting carbon emissions for the good of the planet.

The nation is divided into a series of regional transmission operators and include the SW Power Pool, the Midcontinent Independent System Operator, California, PJM, and ERCOT.

In one way or another, each regional transmission operator (RTO) is interconnected with each of the others except for ERCOT. RTOs were first developed in the 1990s to accommodate the Federal Energy Regulatory Commission's open access declaration. Texas decided to be an introvert. Texas's insularity avoided federal regulation and compromises that other states had to make for the good of their RTO. In addition, Texas through ERCOT was able to make sole decisions that other RTOs weren't able to do such as transmission developed solely to meet Texas's loads. ERCOT is large, really large. It has 46,500 miles of high voltage transmission and schedules 77,000 MW of electricity serving some 24 million customers. Of that total, 16 million can choose their electric provider. I cover customer choice in a bit more detail later.

The freeze that curtailed 48,000 MW of Texas generation and left Brazos with a $1.8 billion bill is due in part to how power plants bid to provide electricity the next day. That's not only true for ERCOT but is also true for other RTOs. It's one of the reasons why Great River Energy decided that $1 was an appropriate price to pay for its 1,100 MW Coal Creek Station. An op-ed written by Ed Hirs for the Washington Post explains it this way:

"ERCOT created a system whereby generators, companies that own power plants, compete by bidding to provide electricity for the day ahead and in real time during the day. It is called an electricity only market. Think of it this way: If the players on the Washington Nationals were paid in the same fashion, only those players on the field for the game that day would earn a paycheck. Everyone else on the roster would be unpaid. Players would offer bids to play for the next day, each undercutting the other.

"Like the Nats in my example, to sell any of their power the generators often bid their power so low that they don't make a profit. Some generators, strapped for cash, began to defer maintenance. Others played an even smarter game by closing power plants or not building new capacity to serve the growing population of Texas. As demand inexorably increased, they could look forward to charging more for their electricity because there was less of it. Really, that is not much different than what Enron did in the California electricity market in 2000 and 2001 except that market manipulation was illegal in California, but not in Texas, thanks to ERCOT. It was all destined to come crashing down and the polar vortex of 2021 was the assault that finally broke the Texas grid."[9]

The New Green Deal, which has yet to pass, didn't freeze the collective asses of Texans as Governor Abbot declared. Renewables, as Abbot also dismissed, didn't cause the Texas electric system to sputter. Then again, renewables aren't going to keep the temperature in check, either. 85 percent of all renewables come from hydropower or burning wood which coal replaced because it was way more efficient. In 2018, wind accounted for 7 percent of the country's cupboard of electrons. Solar hit maybe 2 percent. And yet, many states are counting on those resources to hit their carbon emissions full stop with a goal somewhere within twenty or thirty years.[10] Globally, the wind/solar combo represents 1.1 percent of the world's energy needs.

Oregon Governor Kate Brown supports removing the Snake River Dam, an 1,100 MW hydro while at the same time positing Oregon to be carbon free by 2030. Removing a dam to hasten salmon travel planned by Travelocity to the ocean may be laudable but how can you do that while removing carbon free generation serving some 800,000 homes? That particular question is yet to be answered, leaving the ultimate outcome to the utilities.

Then there's Germany. That country decided to vacate the nuclear and fossil fuel store for what is the renewable one. That switch has cost $36 billion annually and the cost of electricity is 35 cents per kWh. That's the cost for moving from 7 percent devoted to renewables in 2000 to 35 percent in 2019.[11]

Can the world meet the unenforceable Paris Accord to limit warming to less than 2°C?

Lomborg is clear. We won't. Instead, Lomborg writes that we should invest more in research and discovery. Instead, taxpayers across the world paid $141 billion to subsidize inefficient solar and wind energy.[12] Lomborg said that amount of money would produce nearly $93 billion for different green energy. The London School of Economics and Political Science says otherwise. In particular, that article[13] notes that Lomborg, while citing the $141 billion spent on renewable subsidies fails to note that the International Energy Agency bucks up fossil fuel totaling $300 billion.

Lomborg opines, "If we want to change the world, we need to commit to doing things differently and coming up with more ideas because the old ones aren't working."

That includes additional research into:

- Energy storage
- Nuclear power
- Carbon capture and storage
- Seeding the atmosphere
- Imitating Mount Pinatubo which spews 20 million tons of sulfur into the stratosphere, reducing temperature from 1991 to 1993 by.05°C.
- Enacting a carbon tax that discourages carbon production but not at the expense of the world's poor
- Adaptation

The best antidote to reduce climate change, however, is to enrich struggling countries and promote free trade, ensure greater nutrition, greater availability of contraception, health and education, and technology.[14] Which is what NRECA's International Program does. They don't do electrification for the fifty some countries which now have co-ops. Instead, crews from co-ops across the nation teach locals how to hoist and string poles. Others teach boards the principles of governance while stateside co-op personnel show locals the aspects of utility management.

Lomborg is certain the world is unable to meet the 2°C goal by 2100 without expending staggering sums that could better be spent on meeting Maslow's hierarchy of needs. NRECA's International Program is now teaching them the actualization Maslow long favored which is a benefit that far, far exceeds the cost. Except, when it's not. Which is a good place to introduce Joe Baker, the former Mayor of Millington, Tennessee. In 1962, Baker relegated rural America from its once lofty legislative perch to a backwater.

Chapter 10

Baker v. Carr

N umbers are a good place to start, particularly the book in the Old Testament of the same title. Then, God wanted to count the denizens of the Twelve Tribes of Israel. Perhaps impressed with that numeration, the founding fathers insisted in Article I, Section 2 of the US Constitution that the country do the same every ten years. The first census was held in 1790 to decide apportionment or how many Members of Congress each state scored based on population. In 1920, however, while the census was held, Congress stalled the reapportionment until 1929 due principally to the fact that population had shifted from rural to urban. Nearly 14 percent of the population was foreign born, a sentiment that continues to this day. It took Congress nine years to sort it out, just in time for the 1930 census.[1]

State legislatures weren't held to the same standard. Up until 1960, states like Tennessee apportioned state legislative representation by counties. In fact, twenty-eight states guaranteed at least one representative to each county or town in their states.[2] As the 1962 Advisory Commission on Intergovernmental Relations, Apportionment of State Legislatures notes, "In most simple terms, it is the granting of greater representation to rural or sparsely populated areas."[3] The 150 page report also made this astonishing observation:

> "Reapportionment should not be thought of solely in terms of a conflict of interests between urban and rural areas. In the long run, the interest of all is an equitable system of representation that will strengthen state government and is far more important than any temporary advantage to an area enjoying overrepresentation."[4]

Which nobody has said since. Why should they? Maryland was still using districts drawn in 1867. Even states that had constitutions requiring equal population districts were ignoring them. Florida, Georgia, and New Mexico gave small counties 100 times the legislative power of the most populous ones. Decades ago in California, Amador County with a population 14,294 had the same representation in the state's senate as Los Angeles County which had a population of over six million.

"They justified it because that was a cultural norm; it was just the way things were," said Stephen Ansolabehere, a Harvard professor of government. Rural legislators had no incentive to change a system that favored them. "They just let it keep getting worse. You're in power. Why change?"[5]

The immutable fact is that the only constant is change. That wasn't the impetus for a guy by the name of Charles Baker. Fairness was. He lived in Shelby County, Tennessee, home to Graceland. Baker also served as the mayor of Millington, near Memphis. Despite the fact the Tennessee Constitution required legislative districts to be redrawn after each census, the Tennessee legislature, charged with that task, somehow overlooked their responsibility for, oh, nearly sixty years. Doing their job, of course, potentially meant that minorities, particularly African Americans, would gain greater representation in state legislatures. Even more vexing, the concerns of rural Tennessee would be eclipsed by Memphis and Nashville as co-ops would learn when Nashville Congressman Jim Cooper went after them for various misdeeds.

Baker sued Joe Carr, who was the Tennessee Secretary of State. The case finally found its way to the US Supreme Court which uttered this phrase: "One man, one vote." Two years later, the Court in another case rejected an Alabama apportionment which selected the state senate based on area. Chief Justice Warren, the architect of Brown v. Topeka Board of Education, among the most famous of all Supreme Court decisions, nonetheless said Baker v. Carr was the most important case decided during his tenure. And then the era of rural dominance was over in Congress and in State legislatures.

The 2020 Congressional Research Service reported that twenty-two Members of the House are farmers or cattle ranchers.[6] Agrarian states like Illinois, Ohio, Michigan, and even California lost a House seat after the 2020 census was calculated. The equalizer, of course, is the senate, in which each state has two votes no matter the population and the reason why Waxman-Markey was never entertained by the US Senate after the House passed it in 2009.

None of that is particularly new. It's likely the reason NRECA created Co-ops Vote which was designed to inform members on the key issues facing electric co-ops and encourage them to vote and support their co-ops and the communities they serve when they go to the polls. It's why NRECA's political action committee called Action Committee for Rural Electrification or ACRE, with its 36,000 members, is so vitally important. It's why NRECA rolled out Consumers for Political Action which enlists some 11,000 co-op members in ACRE. To that, NRECA and many statewides have grassroots coordinators designed to rile up the locals over adverse legislation. Basin Electric went so far as to identify buddies of legislators across their nine-state service area who might be called upon to lean on their legislative pal should the occasion require. NRECA also once featured "adopt a Member of Congress" which saw statewides schedule meetings with Members representing mostly urban districts until most of them said they were only going to meet with constituents.

All in all, NRECA has done as well as could be expected to stem the loss of legislative prestige leaking every decade from the rural reaches its co-op members serve. The American Public Power Association, which represents the 2,200 municipally owned utilities, is better poised to press for what was once considered conventional energy among the cities and towns in APPA's fold that includes Nashville, Seattle, Los Angeles, and other metropolitan areas. Except they're not, given the environmental bent of those constituent cities that, in the case of California and Washington, have either banned or enacted major roadblocks to any CO_2-inspired kWh crossing their borders. APPA's major city members have formed a large public power council which on occasion pursues issues that might be antithetical to the parent association. The same, by the way, is true with NRECA which has seen Minnesota-based Connexus depart. That 130,000-member co-op contends that NRECA only represents issues important to the little co-ops. Members of G&T, notably Tri-State, are questioning the value of NRECA which they see siding with the G&T over the members looking to exit the G&T. Increasingly, membership in major trade associations, be they NRECA or the NRA, are suffering the same fate as churches over their version of doctrine.

The doctrine of large numbers, however, is immutable. Despite the efforts by states like Georgia to restrict voting rights, along with forty-two other states that have introduced hundreds of bills to increase the level of difficulty of voting, the courts eventually will say otherwise. Electric cooperatives best take notice.

In 1991, the Minnesota legislature took notice of co-op voting districts which showed a wide divergence of population from one district to the next. Co-op directors affected by the eventual legislation requiring districts to be within 10 percent population of each other caused one director to suggest the Minnesota Rural Electric Association lobbyist, Lee Sundberg, should die over that co-op version of Baker v. Carr. Happily, Lee choose otherwise and was much cherished for his legislative representation.

Legislatures, as their wont, tend to nose around in everyone's business. All it takes is one constituent, like a Charles Baker, to ask why his or her co-op district isn't aligned, or why he or she doesn't see directors of color even though the co-op serves a large African American or Hispanic population, or why co-op members are burdened with coal-based energy they don't want?

It would be best if co-ops ask those questions now because co-op solutions are generally better than ones foisted by legislatures or courts.

Chapter 11

The Ties that Bind:

The All-Requirement Contract

The Inception of the All-Requirement Contract

In 1986, Pacific Power and Light successfully acquired the Wyoming-based Shoshone Electric after that co-op's board of directors changed the bylaws to make it much easier to purchase. Shoshone was formed in 1942. The some 2,000-member co-op would later join Tri-State in 1958 six years after the G&T's formation. The contract which bound Shoshone to Tri-State, as was true with the other co-ops and rural public power districts located in Colorado, Nebraska, and Wyoming required the members to purchase all their power from Tri-State. New Mexico co-ops would join in the 1990s when the Albuquerque-based Plains Electric G&T merged with Tri-State.

The all requirements contract was a stipulation from REA (later renamed in the 1990s as the Rural Utility Service or RUS) that loans to build generation and transmission required, as the United States Court of Appeals for the Tenth Circuit, which heard the appeal from the District Court of Wyoming between Tri-State and PP&L, that: "Tri-State distribution cooperatives are required to contract all their energy requirements through Tri-State."[1] The Court also noted that those power purchases had to last as long as the loan requirements with REA.

Pacific Power and Light argued that once it acquired Shoshone Electric, the co-op's obligation to Tri-State ended. The courts disagreed saying if Shoshone left without paying its long-term power contract, others like Garland Power, another Wyoming co-op being wooed by PP&L, would do likewise so as to avoid long-term requirements contracts."[2] The court then added a second point affirming the validity of the all-requirements contract and asserting that REA not only depends on a favorable outcome for Tri-State and, take note, "…but also, the customers of electrical cooperatives across the nation. It would be difficult, if not impossible, to compensate that pervasive injury through damages."

The third point REA made that resonated with the courts was this:

"Moreover, Tri-State argues, allowing Shoshone to take advantage of the REA loan system at both its and Tri-State's level and then to sell out to Pacific constitutes an abuse of the federal program.[3]"

Pay attention to this observation which is at the heart of why REA was created.

"The REA was formed to provide electric power to markets that were not attractive to private entities. Indeed, Shoshone probably would not exist if it were not for subsidies received through the REA. Those subsidies are represented not only by loans to Shoshone, but also by loans to Tri-State. The federal government has, in effect, made it possible for Shoshone to provide electric power to its members. If Pacific is now allowed to purchase Shoshone's assets, it may be obtaining a federal subsidy without meeting the qualifications for such subsidy. At the very least, it may be purchasing both assets supported by federal dollars and a ready-made market created by a federal program without paying adequate compensation."[4]

Five years later, Pacific Corp paid $22.5 million to Tri-State to settle Shoshone's all-requirement contract obligations to Tri-State. The ruling also required PP&L to purchase a modicum of juice from the G&T and agree not to buy any more Tri-State members. Tri-State members signed a compact that said any Tri-State member had the first right to purchase another member entertaining a sell-out offer.

Which pretty much put to rest restive co-op efforts to seek other power suppliers. That era of captivity or coziness, depending on rate increases and lasting some twenty years, ended in 2005.

Initial Assault on Contract Captivity

Another effort to circumscribe the all-requirements contract ensued when the Minnesota-based Great River Energy, a G&T providing power to twenty-eight co-ops ranging in size from 130,000 to 5,000 members, allowed its members to fix their new load growth with a different power supplier. Wright-Hennepin Electric and Minnesota Valley Electric, serving the outer rings of Minneapolis with combined residential accounts exceeding 50,000 members, did so in 2012.[5] Both co-ops chose Basin Electric as their supplemental supplier. Later, eight other GRE members would do similarly with all going sweet on Basin Electric.

At the outset, Basin's rates were far more favorable than GRE whose rates expanded due to the addition of the 99 MW coal-based Spiritwood plant. The Basin rate differential would soon change, showing again that rate advantages could soon dissipate when G&Ts make ill-advised investments like the Dakota Gasification Company.

The Bastion of Basin

Basin Electric was formed in 1961 as a super G&T in order to provide base load generation to other G&Ts and which came to include Tri-State, East River Electric, Central Montana, L&O, Upper Missouri, Central Power, Cornbelt, Northern Iowa Power Cooperative (NIPCO), and a consortium of co-ops called District 9 that fixed new loads on Basin. All told, literally eleven directors represent the interests of the 119 electric co-ops that receive power from Basin which made them, as well, intertwined with the Dakota Gasification Project.

Here's how Basin CEO Paul Sukut, in testimony before the Senate Committee on The Environment and Public Works in February 2019, described Basin's acquisition of that Plant:[6]

"Originally designed to solely produce synthetic natural gas following the 1970s energy crisis, the Dakota Gasification Company has diversified its product stream after acquiring the facility from the Department of Energy in 1988. Today, nearly 80 percent of the plant's revenue is derived from products other than synthetic natural gas. In the process, the Dakota Gasification Company returned over $1 billion of the Federal Government's original investment in the plant through revenue sharing and surrender of tax credits. Notably, the facility is also one of the largest CO2 sequestration projects in the world. Approximately three million tons of CO2 are separated annually during the process of reforming raw gasified coal into pipeline-quality natural gas. Since 2000, more than 35 million tons of CO2 have been shipped via pipeline to the Weyburn oil field in Saskatchewan and utilized for enhanced oil recovery."

"Ill-advised," is a transitory judgement. When Basin contemplated purchasing DGC back in the 1980s, it did so to prevent the potential stranding of 100 MW of load. Basin was worried that if another entrant took title, it would cash out the then existing tax credits and leave the plant rusting on the North Dakota prairie. Basin Electric, then on the wrong side of demand with too little demand and too much supply, simply couldn't afford to orphan an additional 100 or so MW particularly when the wholesale market wasn't as defined as it is today. The early investment paid handsomely when the price of a barrel of oil was ascending and making huge dough for the G&T. Those salad days lasted until 2005 when oil, that is, black crude, North Dakota tea arrived.[7]

Not emphasized in that 2019 testimony was that the price of natural gas had bottomed out thanks to the discovery of natural gas located deep in North Dakota's Bakken formation. At one time, land spread over natural gas land was thought to be only worthwhile for the resumption of the once thriving buffalo herds. Bakken-produced gas is at least 5–18 times cheaper than synthetic gas. Nor did Sukut mention that DGC lost $94 million in 2016[8] or that Basin increased rates 22 percent to offset DGC losses.[9] Those rate impacts caused McKenzie Electric, whose wholesale provider was Upper Missouri, to file suit. Here's what the Minot Daily News had to say:

"In its complaint filed in Northwest District Court, McKenzie Electric states Basin lost $600 million or more since 2013 from "it's unreasonable and imprudent operation of a for-profit synthetic fuels subsidiary." As operated by Basin, the gasification plant produces natural gas so costly that it can be sold only at a loss and Basin's strategy for addressing the problem has been to invest more than $700 million in a urea plant designed to use the natural gas from the gasification facility making the problem worse according to the complaint.[10]

Basin's attorneys dismissed the lawsuit saying, again, according to the Minot Daily News:

"McKenzie Electric is bound by long-term contracts through at least 2075 that preclude it from purchasing power elsewhere. The complaint states that when McKenzie Electric requested a buyout figure from Upper Missouri and Basin, Basin refused to provide one which McKenzie Electric considers a breach of Basin's duty of good faith and fair dealing."

Particularly galling to the co-op, is Basin's continued refusal to allow McKenzie, or any of their members for that matter, to review minutes or financial analyses of DGC. In a brief filed in the District Court, NW Judicial District, November 2019:[11]

"McKenzie contends North Dakota law only allows Basin to charge rates sufficient 'but only sufficient' to meet the cost of operating its generating facilities and not imprudent investments in the continued operation of DGC. McKenzie also demanded access to the Basin board's minutes and those of its committees in addition to financial statements, financial projections, board packets, rate decisions, and other material documents."

While it's never been codified, Cooperative Principle 2 calls for Democratic control or, as described by the National Cooperative Business Association,

"Members control their business by deciding how it's run and who leads it." To date, Basin's attorneys have rejected all information requests and the requested cost for McKenzie to buy out of the long-term contract.

Basin could argue, as they've likely done in other forums, that the G&T made a sizable investment to allow McKenzie to serve the Baaken reservoir oil load. They made such an argument for Mountrail-Williams and, it should be noted, they have not squawked about much of anything.

The disagreements about the all-requirement contracts were mostly rate-related. In the 1990s, climate change or, as it was known then as global warming, was largely dismissed by the nation's G&Ts. Minnkota, a Grand Forks, North Dakota-based G&T, was particularly vociferous in its denunciation of carbon emissions being responsible for raising the world's temperature to untenable heights. Minnkota, among others, funded The Greening Earth Society[12] which operated out of the offices of the Western Fuel Association. Western Fuels CEO, Fred Palmer, acting in a similar capacity for the Greening Earth Society, would later be a senior executive for Peabody Coal. "We can produce more" was essentially the rationale for carbon emissions spouted by The Greening Earth Society.

Trampling Tri-State

If there was a watershed moment for opposition to coal-based generation, at least in Colorado, it came when the city of Boulder, home to the University of Colorado, voted to municipalize Xcel's facilities largely because the multi-state IOU had coal in its energy mix. In 2011, Boulder residents voted to kick out Xcel[13] in favor of a municipal-owned electric utility, a decision that may be finalized with the city's decision to pay Xcel some $94 million for the IOU's facilities. Certainly, that had to be among the reasons why co-ops either energized or, sensing the sentiment of their members, followed suit given that Tri-State's reliance on coal was about 50 percent of that G&T's energy portfolio.

Whether they agreed that coal was largely responsible for climate change, G&T members were stuck with that philosophy and their energy supply but it all changed in 2016. Thirty-six years after the Shoshone litigation firmly cemented the sanctity of the all-requirement contracts, an electrical engineer turned that long-standing decision on its head.

The all-requirements contract was undone by a 30,000-member co-op located in Taos, New Mexico called the Kit Carson Electric Cooperative. The co-op's CEO Luis Reyes long agitated to break away from their power supplier, Tri-State. Between 2000 and 2016, Kit Carson saw twelve rate increases from its power supplier. What's not known is why Tri-State chose to allow Kit Carson to skedaddle although efforts by Kit Carson to have the State of New Mexico regulate Tri-State may have been a contributing factor. Whatever the reasons, Tri-State stated the value of the all-requirements contract was in excess of $163 million. Here's how the Taos News depicted the final negotiated price:

"The $37 million to buy out of a long-term power contract was fronted by Kit Carson Electric Cooperative's new power supplier. Co-op CEO Luis Reyes told The Taos News that Guzman Renewable Energy Partners paid the $37 million exit fee to Tri-State Generation and Transmission. The fee was negotiated as part of a deal to end a contract that was not set to expire until 2040. The ten-year contract with Guzman went into effect July 1. Reyes said the buyout would be paid back by a higher cost for electricity. He said the contract specifies exactly what the cost of power will be for the next ten years but that Guzman requested that the price be kept confidential. Reyes did say the cost will be comparable to Tri-State's current rates until the $37 million is paid off. He said that would take five and one-half years. Kit Carson customers paid Tri-State an average of 7.26 cents per kilowatt-hour in 2015. Based on the co-op's energy sales that year, members would pay an extra 2.31 cents per kilowatt-hour until the buyout money is paid back.

"Making the deal even more attractive to Kit Carson was the ten-year contract with Guzman Renewable Energy Partners. The ten-year contract was fixed, saving the co-op some $50 million over what they would pay Tri-State. Guzman would also supply 35 MW of solar, far eclipsing what Tri-State would have allowed under the terms of its contract with Kit Carson."[14]

FERC Prescription

In 2020, Delta-Montrose followed suit.

Before trafficking in co-ops looking to leave the beating MW breast that is Tri-State, we will talk a bit about the Federal Energy Regulatory Commission or FERC. FERC regulates the transmission and wholesale price of electricity, investigating energy markets along with its jurisdiction of the natural gas industry. FERC does not regulate electric cooperatives that are financed by RUS, leaving that to the states, which raises an issue the Colorado-based Delta-Montrose made in June 2015 asserting that FERC could, if not should, regulate Tri-State.

Delta-Montrose argued that FERC has jurisdiction of co-ops who sell over 4 million MWh which limits their jurisdiction to mostly G&Ts like Tri-State. That G&T demurred saying the 4 million MWh threshold is limited not to Tri-State but to its individual members, all of whom fell well below that particular hurdle. In addition, Tri-State dismissed Delta-Montrose's contention that contractually it was not a member of Tri-State and noted that the patronage capital Tri-State will owe that co-op and its other forty-four members made them so. FERC agreed with Tri-State on those counts and dismissed Delta-Montrose's efforts to place the G&T under FERC jurisdiction[15] which made a Tri-State decision nearly five years later a bit curious.

In 2019, Delta-Montrose approached the Colorado Public Utility Commission (PUC) to achieve a more favorable ruling on what its exit fee should be from Tri-State in order to satisfy its all-requirements contract.[16] In response, Tri-State asked FERC to regulate its rate instead of the PUC and to include what Delta-Montrose, among other Tri-State members agitating to leave, should pay to satisfy the all-requirements contract. Doing so would preclude the PUC along with the New Mexico, Nebraska, and Wyoming regulatory commissions from making that decision. That logic prompted Colorado PUC Commissioner Koncilja to accuse Tri-State of forum shopping.[17] To qualify for FERC oversight, Tri-State had to add a member that was not a co-op or another public power provider. The additions turned out to be quizzical. MIECO, a natural gas wholesaler, provided fuel to Tri-State. Ellgen Ranch rents land from a Tri-State subsidiary. Olson's is a greenhouse operation that purchases thermal energy from the association. United Power, also looking to discard its collection of Tri-State jackets and hats, said those additions "were part of a conspiracy since they all had prior business dealings with Tri-State.[18]

Tri-State's maneuvering apparently was all for naught as FERC made a ruling in March of 2020 for LaPlata Electric Association, yet another Colorado co-op telling Tri-State that if they loved them, then they should let them go. LaPlata brought their beef before the Colorado PUC. They are a 34,000-member co-op located in Durango, Colorado and they had this to say:[19]

> "We are thrilled our complaint against Tri-State can proceed to a formal hearing so we can obtain a just, fair, and reasonable exit charge," said Jessica Matlock, LPEA CEO. "Since we don't have an exit number, we can't determine the best course of action for our members. LPEA has a strategic goal to reduce carbon 50 percent by 2030 while remaining cheaper than 70 percent of our Colorado cooperative peers. To achieve that, we have to explore every option available."

Meanwhile, Delta-Montrose negotiated its exit fee from Tri-State. Here are those details as reported by the Colorado Sun:

> "Under the exit agreement, which would have DMEA leave Tri-State on June 30, the cooperative would pay a $62.5 million exit fee, and $26 million for local Tri-State infrastructure. They would also forgo the $48 million in equity the cooperative held as a member of Tri-State. The DMEA/Tri-State agreement still must be submitted for final approval by the Federal Energy Regulatory Commission which is now the regulator for Tri-State. A number of Tri-State cooperatives have chafed under the association's long-term contracts that limit local generation to 5 percent of demand as they hoped to add more renewable generation. DMEA's contract ran to 2040. Tri-State was also criticized for still being heavily dependent on coal-fired generation."[20]

The Colorado Sun added:

"The $88.5 million will be paid by DMEA or a third party according to Tri-State. When the Kit Carson Electric Cooperative in Taos, New Mexico left Tri-State in 2016, its new electric wholesaler, Guzman Energy, paid the $37 million exit fee which it is recouping in the first few years of its contract with the co-op. DMEA has about 28,000 members and Kit Carson has 29,000 but DMEA has more commercial and industrial members and about twice the electricity demand as Kit Carson with an annual peak of 95 to 100 megawatts according to Virginia Harman, a DMEA spokeswoman. DMEA is in the final steps of completing a twelve-year wholesale power purchase agreement with Guzman Energy, Harman said, adding that there would be no further comment until the agreement is completed."[21]

None of the machinations were lost on Tri-State's remaining forty-one members located in New Mexico, Nebraska, Colorado, and Wyoming. Here's what Tim Lindall, former CEO of Wheat Belt Public Power District located in Sidney, Nebraska, home to some 5,110 customers, said:

"In late March 2020 the FERC ruled that it had nearly full jurisdiction over Tri-State's rates. The FERC also ruled in Wheat Belt's favor that the Class A wholesale rate was not just and reasonable or cost based and ordered Tri-State and Wheat Belt to enter refundable settlement negotiations at the FERC. Our intent is not to break our contract with Tri-State, but rather protect our rate payers from other states, and from other members who game the system, and we desire to hold Tri-State to a level of FERC accountability to protect us all in the future. I never would have believed that I would have advocated for federal oversight ten years ago, however, in today's world, the small guy needs to be ensured a fair playing field."[22]

Not long after Lindall left to manage a co-op in Kansas, Wheat Belt joined in the effort to file walking papers from Tri-State. While that public power district has yet to strolled, Wheat Belt's challenge resulted in a 2 percent reduction. Other Nebraska PPDs served by the Nebraska Public Power District have rates that are about a third less.

The small guy impact was exactly the manifestation Tri-State attempted to make when United Power in the summer of 2020 made its case to see Tri-State in its collective rear-view mirror. The co-op, numbering some 93,000 members, is the G&T's largest member. Coincidently, in 1987 United, then called Union, was the target of a takeover effort by Public Service of Colorado. Thanks to the CFC Integrity Fund and a nationwide effort of door knockers fueled by co-op volunteers, United fended off that acquisition effort. In July of 2020, United made its case to break away from their G&T which, oddly enough, sees the United Power website brag about their collaborative effort with Tri-State. In another bit of irony, United relied on NERA Consulting, the same firm used to question the economics of addressing environmental issues, the very ones departing Tri-State members cited in that PUC divorce case.

In the United Power case, the Colorado administrative law judge agreed with the co-op's methodology which included dough the Denver-based co-op owes on existing fossil fuel plants along with solar and wind generation. Subtracted from that total is the amount Tri-State owes United in patronage dividends, a formula comparable to that used by Kit Carson and Delta Montrose. Tri-State argued United Power's share is around $762 million. The price of goodbye set by the administrative law judge was $25 million.[23] Tri-State said that would leave more than $1 billion in unjust costs split among the remaining members across Tri-State's four-state area and would underscore the Wheat Belt CEO's laments.

Happily, for Tri-State and perhaps its other members, the Colorado PUC admitted that the addition of MEICO,[24] which supplies gas for Tri-State's gas-fired turbines and along with the garden center which would be sure to be supplying centerpieces at the next Tri-State annual meeting dinner, was sufficient to land Tri-State under the jurisdiction of FERC. That decision keeps United within the Tri-State family which also includes the disaffected LaPlata Electric.

Those departures and fidgety member co-ops and PPDs led the Tri-State board to adopt a far more flexible energy plan which not only allows its members to exceed the 5 percent imposition on new renewable sources but, as Tri-State CEO Duane Highley said, the plan also does this:

"The Responsible Energy Plan announced in January 2020, positions Tri-State as a leader in the clean energy transition and to effectively comply with federal and state regulations. Under the plan, 50 percent of the energy our cooperative consumes will come from renewable resources by 2024. This new contract option will allow our utility members to self-supply up to 50 percent of their energy demand, subject to availability in the open season. This is in addition to a new program that expands opportunities for members to participate in community solar gardens."[25]

It appears that the reason for those all-requirement contracts to secure RUS loans for coal-based generation have lost that particular generation luster as seen by the Minnesota-based Great River Energy decision to shutter its 1,100 MW Coal Creek Station facility which has been operating for some forty years. That plant and others owned and operated by Big Rivers (Kentucky), GRE, Basin Electric (East Kentucky), Hoosier (Indiana), and Buckeye Power (Ohio) caused them to drop their subscription to Mother Jones Magazine which rated them in 2015 as the "most carbon-intense power plants in the nation."[26]

According to GRE, their 2,200 MW Coal Creek plant is losing some $170 million annually amid "market challenges as the plant competes with cheap natural gas and renewable energy."[27] Gas, of course, was thought to be on the brink of extinction as late as 1978 when the Fuel Use Act was passed and renewable energy was thought to peak when windmills churned water from the depths. Long-term contracts have long-term decisions which, in the case of coal-based generation loans, also reflect the number one song from 1978, "You Light up my Life," by Debby Boone.[28]

Not that Ms. Boone should have the final lyrical say, but perhaps Jeff Nelson, retired CEO of the South Dakota-based East River Electric, past chair of the Midwest Electric Consumers Association Board, member of South Dakota Cooperative Hall of Fame and Engineering-like Cooperstown Hall, and current director on the South Dakota investment council has to say, particularly in light of what consultant Steve Collier said earlier, "If we didn't already have G&Ts today, we wouldn't form them. The landscape is totally changed due to competitive wholesale power markets. The G&Ts only survive because of their all-requirements contracts, not because they are doing everything that they can to be relevant and competitive."

Here are Jeff Nelson's musings:

"The concept of pledging repayment of monies borrowed for an agreed upon purpose over a set time period is not controversial, until it can't be repaid. Those members who have left Tri-State are trading Tri-State for a new form of all-requirements contractors namely, Guzman Partners.

"The real question is how can distribution co-ops better capture the value of new technology and energy markets without changing the old structure of G&T's?

"It's a complex question and one that in my view rests on the simple formula that always makes co-ops succeed or fail, namely building trust focused on the best long-term outcome for the member. G&T's emerged as a tool to achieve badly needed scope and scale for distribution retailers who early on concluded market strength demanded more scope and scale to compete and survive. Thus G&T's and then CFC, Federated, NISC, ACE Power marketing, National Renewable Energy Organization. But the failure to convince the KCs and DMs and the GRE members, who fixed the model, rested on the loss of confidence of their G&T sticking to meeting the needs of the members. Thus, the private equity crowd and smart power marketers have been able to succeed, thereby undercutting Tri-State at least in the short term.

"G&T's need to help their members be agents for change. Hybrid solutions can be within G&T's such as offering tools for market access for their member's end customers who want market access or to develop renewables etc. In other words, the G&T's could build their own mini Guzman Partners and fund it not with private equity but by letting members invest equity, using CFC or CoBank debt capital and thereby creating mini trading desks to tailor market access for large or other users which want such status. The traditional all-requirements contract doesn't have to be a barrier to those kinds of solutions unless it is used as a shield by the G&T to preserve the status quo and to protect the G&T rather than genuinely working for the best interests of the co-op member.

"With a future of uncertainty and being the very smallest of the small in the universe of electric utilities, G&Ts need to provide scope and scale may have to be relearned. There will not be that chance, however, if the G&Ts aren't willing to be a part of the solution."[29]

Denouement means the final part of a play, movie, or narrative in which the strands of the plot are drawn together and matters are explained or resolved. Literally it means to untie after the climax when the problems faced by the characters begin to resolve. In the drama that is Tri-State, FERC in late fall 2020 said it has exclusive jurisdiction over Tri-State's rates and, more to the point, "member system exit charges."[30] For United, FERC's decision superseded any decision the Colorado PUC might have considered. While that keeps the remaining Tri-State family together, Tri-State now is assuredly regulated by FERC in an arena that up till now was mostly the playing field for investor-owned utilities. To that, the favorable Dairyland decision handed down in the 1960s by the Federal Power Commission, the forerunner to FERC, said it did not have jurisdiction over co-ops because as the LaCrosse, Wisconsin-based Dairyland Power claimed, it was already regulated by its federal lender, the RUS which has fallen out of favor.

At least for now.

Chapter 12

G&T Governance Course

You would have great difficulty seeing any trade association offering more governance training than NRECA. Surprisingly, none of that training is offered for G&T boards.

Governance of electric cooperatives, private power companies, corporations, and LLCs are a growth industry. The National Association of Corporate Directors, for example, pulls in some $34 million derived from governance workshops.[1] Amazon counts more than 50,000 book titles on governance in their library. Perhaps most notable, which set NRECA on its extensive course on governance, was then NRECA's Director of Education Bob Kabat early decision to hire the legendary business sage Peter Drucker to advise NRECA on governance and business practices. By then Drucker was world famous for assisting Japan after World War Two to revitalize that country's war-torn businesses. Sony, Honda, and other Japanese businesses were the result. Kabat chose well and his legend is the reason the Management Internship Program located in Madison, Wisconsin is named the "Robert Kabat Management Internship Program.

Alfred Sloan, who ran General Motors from 1923 to 1956 and retired three years after the first Corvette was introduced, once observed, "Gentlemen, I take it that we are all in complete agreement on the decision here. Then, I propose that we postpone further discussion to give ourselves time to develop disagreement and perhaps gain some understanding of what the decision is all about."[3]

Given the current fact that most G&T boards of directors are old, white, male, and more in tune with the 1976 Fuel Act instead of, say, the New Green Deal, smarting up G&T boards should represent a new urgency. To wit, here are nine issues that an envisioned course might include:

1. At the outset, a board needs to have a clear understanding of what its function is. Representing the home co-op provides perspective on what the locals may want, yet that may not be what the function is of the G&T. Beyond that is the two hats doctrine that says while you may hail from yonder, your duty is to the G&T. That may be a difficult concept especially when a director is asked why they voted this way or that at his or her distribution meeting.

2. First and foremost, what value does a director bring? It is perhaps prejudicial but one Midwest co-op CEO opined that directors elected to represent the G&T co-ops were selected on the basis of geography so as to avoid paying for additional mileage. As it is, most G&T boards are comprised of directors, not CEOs, who do not have a power supply acumen as does a CEO. The bromide that managers manage and directors direct is hardly a beatitude given that nearly 70 percent of a co-op's cost is due to power supply.

3. It was the distribution co-ops in the 1950s, 1960s, and 1970s that developed the G&T based on economies of scale. It made great sense then but departing co-ops today think otherwise. There is no appropriate exit fee given the financial obligations of the long-term power contract, the value of accumulated capital credits, and the value of money to mention but a few of the variables needing answers before a co-op can skip from their obligations. Consulting firms, particularly those that are prying members away from Tri-State, provide information which likely is skewed toward their clients. NRECA and, in particular, CFC and CoBank—which may well have provided loan funds to a G&T—should also cover mechanics of the costs of leaving.

4. All G&T boards are insular. Their boards are comprised of either a director or a CEO and mostly the former. To ensure greater representation, G&Ts and co-op boards should allow for outside directors who represent commercial or industrial loads and who provide diversity that is now lacking. Some aspect of the Sarbanes-Oxley rule should be incorporated to provide a financial expert as a board member and to engage dissidents whose views may

be askance of the board majority but whose views nonetheless are enlightening.

5. G&T's original purpose was to provide power supply either through contracts or building base load resources. The new mission is to assist co-ops that want to supplant coal-based generation with more renewable sources. After all, the G&T's enduring strength is developing economies of scale.

6. G&Ts should allow their members much greater latitude beyond the current 5 percent to source renewable energy, similar to what Tri-State has done. Participating co-ops have a membership base that may be able to provide renewable resources be it solar, digesters, wind, battery storage, etc., as a twenty-first century PURPA designed to enlist the membership. Limiting what the ultimate member can provide does disservice to the cooperative model.

7. G&Ts should contemplate how to shed long-term commitments. RUS long-term loans for generation total about $14 billion with probably a similar outlay from CFC and CoBank. Years ago, GRE prepaid its RUS debt and now relies on private financing. Other G&Ts should think similarly or NRECA should consider legislation forgiving that debt with the mandate that coal-based generation be replaced largely with renewable energy.

8. When does it make sense to be regulated either by the Federal Energy Regulatory Commission, a state's PUC, or neither. Regulation, of course, presents more than two sides of the sword but boards should have a clear understanding of the upside of regulation beyond the usual banal response of, "We don't want it."

9. There are looming dangers to holding on to coal-based generation. That includes the potential of losing insurance, legislative action, intrusion of third-party providers, legal action, and all the issues confronting coal-based holdings.

There are more issues undoubtedly to cover, but ignoring these, allows others to dictate the terms affecting G&Ts which surely must be the province of NRECA.

Chapter 13

Can We Do It Again?

The "Electric Cooperative Purpose: A Compass for the 21st Century," asks early on, "Can we do it again?" A challenge, or perhaps a lament, made by virtually every sports team that has captured a title of some sort. The answer, short of the Yankees and the 94-95 Nebraska Cornhuskers, is not often.

Co-ops have more optimism for affirming that inquiry. Then again, co-ops have defined service territories, only a modicum of regulation, the ability to define line extension terms and disconnect policies, and deciding when, if ever, to kick back capital credits. Do it again[1] sounds more like that Steely Dan song, recycling old habits and reflecting an observation from the 21st Century Cooperative Committee:

> "A cooperative that is just a group of employees providing services with an increasingly passive and unengaged member-ownership is not functioning as a true cooperative."[2]

Recall that the report said connecting with 15 percent of the membership is a tipping point to "energize the larger membership." By comparison, it takes 68 percent to sell the co-op. So how can co-ops, as the report notes,[3] "find opportunities to work face to face with groups of their member-owners.?"

How did the early framers do it in the 1930s? They met to discuss fulfilling an unmet need, rural electrification. Here's what you might consider in this century: climate change.

NRECA statistics show co-ops cover 56 percent of America's landmass. That's a lot of acres of land tilled and toiled by co-op Boards that still include mostly ranchers and farmers.[4]

Massachusetts is one of three states with no co-ops, but it is the home of Indigo that launched an initiative to sequester 1 trillion metric tons of carbon dioxide.[5] Growers who join can net $15 per ton of carbon sequestered. Dakota Gasification Company, owned by Basin Electric, captures about 2.5 to 3 million metric tons of CO2 annually.[6] Said in a different way, a trillion metric tons, also known as a terraton, is one million billion tons which dwarf a bit of Basin's heralded sequestration effort. Here's how a June 2019 CNBC report described Indigo's goal:[7]

"Indigo Agriculture, the Boston-based start-up that uses natural microbiology to revolutionize the way farmers grow crops, has unveiled a first-of-a-kind program to tackle climate change worldwide. The company launched the Terraton Initiative to accelerate carbon sequestration from agricultural soil on a massive scale. The goal: to capture 1 trillion metric tons (a terraton) of carbon dioxide worldwide from 3.6 billion acres of farmland through a marketplace that gives farmers incentives to implement regenerative farming practices.

"Capturing atmospheric carbon dioxide from agricultural soil is a way to restore soil health while returning carbon levels to those prior to the Industrial Revolution, according to the U.N.'s Intergovernmental Panel on Climate Change.

"Today many environmental experts say agricultural farming emits 25 percent to 35 percent of all CO2 into the atmosphere—more than all modes of transportation combined. The trend has contributed to extreme changes in weather that are reducing crop yields and making livestock more vulnerable to disease. All this threatens the global food supply as demand from a booming global population grows.

"'The potential for agricultural soils to capture and store atmospheric carbon dioxide is the most hopeful solution I know of to address climate change,' said David Perry, Indigo's CEO. 'The technology and know-how for regenerative farming already exists, so we can begin to make a difference right now.'

"Which is why the Biden Administration is considering a multibillion-dollar bank to pay farmers to store carbon in soil.

"'And this can be done on a massive scale,' says Inigo's co-founder and chief innovation officer, Geoffrey von Maltzahn.

"These practices include minimal tillage of the soil, cover cropping, crop rotations, using fewer chemicals and fertilizers, and incorporating livestock grazing. These are all ways to increase soil's carbon content and water retention, so less CO2 is released into the atmosphere.

"As Maltzahn explains, soils play a key role in the carbon cycle by soaking up carbon from dead plant matter. Plants absorb CO2 from the atmosphere through photosynthesis and pass carbon to the ground when dead roots and leaves decompose. But it can cause carbon to be released from the soil at a faster rate than it is replaced. This net release of carbon to the atmosphere contributes to global warming.

"To catalyze the initiative, Indigo is creating the Indigo Carbon marketplace.[8] Growers who join Indigo Carbon for the 2019 crop season are eligible to receive $15 per metric ton of carbon dioxide sequestered.[9]

"In partnership with the Ecosystem Services Market Consortium and other organizations, such as The Rodale Institute and the Soil Health Institute, Indigo will use its digital agronomy capabilities and software imagery analysis to measure and verify soil carbon sequestration and on-farm emission levels."[10]

The Michigan State University Extension June 2007 newsletter contained, "How much carbon dioxide does an acre of Michigan corn absorb in a growing season?"

"That is a question that is often asked, and the answer may surprise many people. Our calculations show that number to be in excess of 36,000 lbs. of carbon dioxide per acre.!"[11]

Using the 1862 Homestead Act, which allocated 160 acres to anyone not convicted of insurrection, the Indigo Carbon Marketplace could conceivably provide $2,400 in carbon payments to cornhuskers. Wheat per acre absorbs 10,000 pounds, hemp is good for twice that, and alfalfa is a bit less at 1,400 pounds per acre.

Carbon markets can be sketchy. The Regional Greenhouse Gas Initiative, covering ten eastern states, saw carbon credits selling for $5.75 based on a June 2020 report.[12] California, the first state to adopt a cap and trade in 2019 reports raising some $12.5 billion in carbon revenues.[13] The latest 2020 report shows a ton of carbon aligned with two oxygens going for $16.84.[14]

All of that sounds promising, except for a discordant note sounded in an admittedly dated 2007 Harper's Magazine article entitled Conning the Climate by Mark Shapario. The author, an investigative reporter, addressed the annual Minnesota Rural Electric Association Energy Issues Summit in 2010. Here's a summary of his presentation based on that article:[15]

"Unlike traditional commodities, which sometimes during the course of their market exchange must be delivered to someone in physical form, the carbon market is based on the lack of delivery of an invisible substance to no one. In an attempt to compensate for this intangibility, the United Nations has certified twenty-six firms worldwide—in U.N. lingo, Designated Operational Entities (DOEs)—to validate the promises of emissions reducers and then to verify, often years later, that those reductions actually occurred.

Validation is also the Achilles heel of the system, and this vulnerability stems in large part from the central requirement for offsets: additionality—that is, proof that one's renewable-energy project would not happen without the capital generated by selling carbon credits. Thus, the process is fraught with obstacles of definition, involving benefits and drawbacks.

In fact, the problems with turning carbon into a commodity begin at the very moment of conception. A one-ton carbon credit is not precisely reproducible like an ounce of gold or twenty tons of pork bellies; each credit emerges from entirely different conditions and components. Each represents a promise of potentially varying longevity and effectiveness, to say nothing of trustworthiness. On paper, cap and trade is seductively elegant; but in practice, making good on its promises would require an enforcement structure that is hardly less onerous than the obvious (if painful) solution to climate change that cap and trade was designed to avoid: that is, a carbon tax."

What is bankable is government largesse, if not the co-ops' all too often forgotten asset, capital credits. Which is a convenient place to couple then East River CEO Jeff Nelson with Section 1603. Pay attention to that very cool idea which, sadly, has expired but the genius behind it is instructive for the 21st Century Cooperative.

According to the US Treasury home page, the Section 1603 program was created as part of the American Recovery and Reinvestment Tax Act of 2009 to increase investment in domestic clean energy production.[16] Under Section 1603, the Department of the Treasury made payments in lieu of investment tax credits to eligible applicants for specified energy property used in a trade or business or for the production of income. The purpose of the 1603 payment was to reimburse eligible applicants for a portion of the cost of installing the specified energy property which covered a bunch of stuff, including wind.

In 1992, Congress provided a Production Tax Credit which started at 1.9 cents per kWh and now is 1.5 cents for that same kilowatt hour. As the term implies, a tax credit offsets an investor's taxable income at 1.5 cents per every kWh the individual's financed turbine churns. Tax credits can also be sold to other investors needing tax breaks.

As Jeff Nelson observed, the American Recovery and Reinvestment Act passed in 2009 was designed both to spur renewable energy and provide upfront financing for small-time energy operators who didn't have sufficient income to take advantage of the PTC.[17] Nelson said in an email, "Section 1603 of the Recovery Act the door opened to small investors if, if the 'deal' could be affordably packaged, and if construction/operations could be assured." However, it was the use of capital credits that first spurred member investment in ethanol plants which was used for the Prairie Wind project.[18] Again, in Nelson's words:

> "We believed we had all the elements available. First as to the financing, East River Electric (and its members) played an elemental role in helping to finance ethanol using the small investor model including offering use of up to $5,000 in unpaid capital credits as zero interest loans to members. That leverage enabled as much as 20 percent of the equity raised for the first wave of producer owner ethanol plants. Thus,

if it worked for ethanol why not wind. It did work and ultimately over $3.5 million of capital credit loans helped launch what turned into a billion dollar plus ethanol industry about doubling corn production in SD. For SD Wind Partners it did work as well.[19]

Here's how it worked in South Dakota according to the American Wind Energy Association:[18]

"Convincing rural South Dakotans to invest in the wind wasn't a problem. Finding a business model for a community-owned sustainable energy project that would benefit rural economies, however, was a different story.

"We asked [potential investors], 'Do you believe the wind is going to blow in South Dakota?' and 'Do you believe people are going to need electricity? We made it simple,' said Jim Headley, a South Dakota rancher and Central Electric Cooperative board member." "If you don't believe these things, you don't want to deal with us."

East River's history of serving rural communities through a cooperative model spurred an interest in bringing a locally owned, sustainable wind project to the state. It hired a consulting company, Val-Add Service Corp, which specializes in assisting new entities to generate business and it was active in the state's ethanol development. East River then approached Basin with the idea of building a separate, locally owned wind project adjacent to Prairie Winds' planned wind facility.

A deal was struck. The project includes a Power Purchase Agreement in which Prairie Winds agreed to purchase the electricity produced at 4.3 cents/kWh and will escalate at 1.5 percent annually. More than $16 million was raised.

"Keep in mind, this was at a time when the economy was at its worse," said East River Electric General Manager Jeffrey Nelson. "We thought, 'Let's start [holding investor meetings] in the area around Crow Lake, then in concentric circles. Once we got to the second or third meeting, people were driving from 200 miles away."[20]

Besides willing local investors, a crucial aspect of the project's success was its ability to take advantage of a cash grant that was part of The American Recovery and Reinvestment Act of 2009. The Section 1603 tax grant paid for 30 percent of the capital cost or $6.7 million. The total SDWP funding was nearly $11 million of debt and $12.5 million for equity which includes the $6.7 million from the federal grant. The final construction cost was $21.5 million which was $1.69 million under budget. Though the project is now complete, replicating that plan would be problematic without the Section 1603 tax grant. It is no longer available to projects with construction dates that began after December 31, 2011. Then again, given the President's insistence on carbon-free electricity, that provision could well come back.

Recall Jim Cooper's criticism of co-ops because of hoarding of capital credits. East River's use of that accumulated member capital was vital to finance both ethanol and wind development for its members who were able to use their capital credits, albeit at a zero-interest loan, to both create jobs and a self-satisfying return on investment. Can we do it again shouldn't be a haunting question. Instead, co-ops and their G&Ts should look at all of the accumulated capital credits with an eye toward using those funds to benefit the members and the co-op community.

To that well of capital, there are a great deal of tax incentives let alone renewable energy largesse from RUS, The Department of Energy, and the US Treasury and including what individual states fork over for the reoccurring kilowatt hour. Your knowledge of those sources may fall short of your aspirations but there is a wealth of organizations to help like the National Renewable Cooperative Organization, USDA State Director, RUS General Field Representative, statewide, NRECA, CFC, CoBank, Congressional offices, and more all waiting to hear your idea. Think about what East River did to answer the question of can we do it again? "Yes, we can." Including, perhaps, rewarding members who reduce their carbon output. That's next.

Chapter 14

Contemplating the Carbon
Individual Retirement Act

L et's return to the genesis of this book, the 21st Century Cooperative Committee, that asked, "Why were cooperatives created in the first place?" Turns out it's the same answer to the question asked eighty-five years ago, "To improve the lives of our members." That seems to be the model for environment-social-governance responsibility investment, the most notable of which is called Climate Action 100.[1] The fund now surpasses some $32 trillion dollars as detailed by retired CFC Governor Sheldon Petersen at a past CFC Financial Forum. Among the societal concerns raised by investors, according to Petersen, is climate change. And well they should. The United Nation's Intergovernmental Panel on Climate Change concluded that we have twelve years[2] to dramatically reduce carbon emissions before really bad things start to happen globally. Back in 1988, NASA scientist, James Hanson, told a Senate Committee that 400 parts per million (ppm) of carbon in the atmosphere was the climate's tipping point. Today, its 415 CO2 ppm.[3]

Smithsonian Magazine reports that the earth loses 1.2 trillion tons of ice each and every year. Climate change based on human activities has warmed the ocean by 22 Fahrenheit.[4] That would be .22 warmer per each decade since 1980. Blame could be attributed to that God-awful song by Air Supply that despoiled transistor radios in the same year, All Out of Love, but, no, it's us. Global sea levels have risen 1.3 inches since 1994. If you're Coos-Curry Electric, which serves a light house located on a spit off the Southern Oregon Coast, you are very worried.

To be sure, cooperatives and others in the electric power industry are on the path toward a substantially less carbon-intensive future. The problem is the transformation from fossil fuels to non-carbon renewable energy is happening way too slowly.

Co-ops, formed to improve the lives of their members, should consider this accelerant: Reward individual actions that reduce a co-op member's carbon footprint by converting the avoided carbon into funds deposited in a retirement account.

The Carbon IRA concept was conceived by Jason Makansi, a long-time power industry professional, independent consultant, and author of *Lights Out: The Electricity Crisis, the Global Economy, and What It Means to You* and the forthcoming book, *Carbon IRA & YouTility: How to Reward Carbon Reduction and Address Climate Change Before It's Too Late* which sees several chapters of that book included elsewhere.

Carbon IRA addresses two seemingly intractable societal problems simultaneously:

- Global climate change
- Inadequate retirement savings

Both are perplexing issues for cooperative member-owners. Fully 86 percent of Americans believe they face a retirement crisis. A similar number are concerned about climate change. More than one-third of your members have less than $50,000 in savings. Many co-op members are immeasurably worried about that and want to limit catastrophic climate change. Young folks with huge college debt burdens are especially at risk.

Twenty-three states have carbon emission reduction goals and several, besides California, are moving to pass cap and trade, carbon taxes, cap and dividends, and other schemes designed to penalize carbon emissions.[5]

Note the focus on penalties. Co-ops can do so much more by rewarding carbon reduction and energy conservation. Here's how:

Electric cooperatives should be natural early adopters of Carbon IRA. They could invest in such programs for their ratepayers. It would create strong incentives for more rapid displacement of fossil fuel-based electricity with renewable energy (solar, hydro, and wind). First, however, co-ops should tell their members how much carbon emission each kWh represents. Coal-based generation already lists carbon emissions per MWh—an average of 2000 pounds—which would equate to two pounds per kWh. Sending environmental signals to your members also allows the co-op to track carbon reductions.

By encouraging their ratepayers to either install rooftop PV or to buy electricity from renewable sources like their generation and transmission cooperative, co-ops could create a strong feedback loop. Customers would buy into long-term contracts for renewable energy, similar to solar gardens, which supports the investment necessary to displace coal and gas-fired power plants with solar and wind which is already mandated throughout most of the United States.

Co-ops plan and invest on a multi-decade basis. Imagine if your customers have committed to renewable electricity purchases on a multi-year basis which is incentivized by retirement fund contributions.

Co-ops track capital credits and have paid out some $1 billion over the years.[6] It's a modest step, not a giant leap, for them to also be agencies that collect retirement funds from carbon avoided by their ratepayers. Homestead Funds would be a logical vehicle for managing the accounts. The monthly utility bill, already a menu of costs, fees, taxes, etc., could serve as a mechanism for tracking avoided carbon, validating it, and reporting it to the entity responsible for managing the retirement account. A utility by design monitors electricity consumption and could easily, by extension, monitor avoided carbon.

Of course, implementing the Carbon IRA framework does pose challenges but they can be addressed. For instance, let's say I want to monetize the avoided carbon for keeping my thermostat at 82°F in the summer. What is my baseline behavior for which that will be compared? Would the authority use the average temperature setting for all of America, the region in which I live, or the average of my last several years of usage?

How do you differentiate between an EV driven in a region with 80 percent renewable electricity in the grid and one with 40 percent? Do you compare the avoided carbon to the average vehicle in America or to the previous car a person drove?

A utility, for example, could determine from having data from thousands of smart thermostats that the average ratepayer setting is 76°F in its service territory. The National Information Solutions Cooperative (NISC) already does that. It could design a sliding scale of carbon value for customers willing to keep the thermostat between 77 and 82°F.

Predictability is also critical so that utilities avoid paying for expensive peaking generation. Ratepayers should be rewarded not only for avoiding carbon by maintaining a higher temperature but also for helping to make the utility's demand more predictable.

Today, many utilities have programs rewarding ratepayers financially for such behaviors. It wouldn't be a stretch to convert those programs so that they reward with funds deposited into a retirement account.

Similar issues would have to be reasoned out for the EV example. Ratepayers who charge their EVs at night when electricity is least expensive should also benefit for avoiding the carbon associated with that electricity. A utility could simply decide that if their electricity generating mix is 50 percent renewable and 50 percent fossil, then EV charging carbon credits can be apportioned respectively.

Perhaps the most important question an early adopter has to answer is, "What is a fair price for avoided carbon?" Perhaps it should simply be to adopt the market price. There is a carbon-trading market just like there are debt, equities (stocks), currencies, and commodities trading mechanisms. Over the last ten years, the price of carbon in those markets has ranged from $5–200 per ton.

Back-of-envelope calculations show that it takes quite an effort for a consumer to avoid a ton of carbon output. If that carbon is priced at the low end of the range, it's not going to result in much of an incentive. At the high end of the range, though, the contribution is far from negligible. And when several behaviors are combined and compounded over the years, the contributions really can lead to a much more affluent retirement!

Given the pressure of the IPCC timeline to climate catastrophe, maybe the better question is not what the market price of carbon is but what is the price commensurate with the threat of irreversible climate change in twelve years and the threat of penniless retirees decade to decade? The fact is, organizations attempt to quantify difficult qualitative parameters and define benchmarks, standards, and methodologies all the time including accountants versed in utility business models, financial planners, and environmental professionals.

Victims of airline disasters, terrorist events such as 9/11, and other calamities are valued in compensation proceedings for families or heirs. Participants in class action lawsuits sue for damages which have to be estimated. Insurance companies pay out for damages, injury, and death based on fuzzy estimates of value. Reparations to victims of political and societal prejudice and racism have to be calculated based on nebulous value concepts.

So, while the market value of a ton of avoided carbon isn't much of an incentive, the threat value based on twelve years to get our collective act in gear could be one or two orders of magnitude larger.

Already carbon-trading markets have been developed and are run by the same financial management firms that manage IRA accounts. If we begin to acknowledge carbon as if it has monetary value, people will adapt their behaviors and consumer habits as if discharging carbon dioxide is tantamount to wasting money.

Think about this. Some economists have a name for a kind of incentive, a nudge, and if you want to learn more, have your co-op CEO read and report on *Nudge: Improving Decisions About Health, Wealth, and Happiness*, by Richard Thaler and Cass R Sunstein.[8]

A nudge, in simple terms, is a carrot and not a stick. It's like the quarter that is taped to a survey you got in the mail and were asked to fill in and return. Or the promise of making a donation to a popular charity if you purchase from such and such company. It's not that the specific donation you created by your action, or the quarter, is so valuable. It's just that you feel better about the action because of the associated nudge.

Behavioral economics has been a thriving field for decades. Psychology gets thrown into the mix. In a pioneering study from decades ago, workers on an assembly line became more productive when the lighting was improved at their workspaces. At first, researchers thought it was because better lighting allowed them to work more efficiently. What they later discovered is that the workers just appreciated not being ignored by management.

There are plenty of good examples of similar incentive programs which are proving successful with consumers. If you are willing to have your driving monitored, auto insurance companies will give you a significant break on your premiums. If you are willing to sacrifice a little comfort on hot summer days by allowing your smart thermostat to be tweaked remotely, some electric utilities will kick back some of the savings in meeting peak loads. Home insurers will give you a break if you have smoke detectors installed.

Some companies even offer vitality credits or breaks on health insurance premiums to employees who monitor their steps with their Fitbit-like device or phone health app. In the case of one electric cooperative, the vitality credits are added to the employee's flexible health spending account.

A detailed explanation of the framework can be found in *Carbon IRA & YouTility: How to Address Climate Change & Reward Carbon Reduction Before It's Too Late*, by Jason Makansi. Makansi prefers to call the Carbon IRA as shove economics only because the urgency of addressing climate disruption is way beyond nudges.

Chapter 5 detailed the new electric retailers called Community Choice Aggregators or CCA and defined them as an "electric co-op buyers club."[7] Shouldn't that electric buying club be us? Community Choice Aggregators consciously, or not, are emulating what are and remain the best part of a cooperative. Perhaps that explains the traction CAA is having in seven states including Illinois, Ohio, California, and New Jersey. Those state communities now offer renewable energy to amenable customers who are paying the incumbent utility for the use of their distribution facilities for delivery. Other co-op-centric states including Colorado, New Mexico, Oregon, Arizona, and Nevada are considering enabling legislation. Ignoring the reason why co-ops were formed—to improve the lives of their members—leads to other options in an increasingly competitive marketplace.

In 1974, the Employee Retirement Income Security Act (ERISA) created individual retirement accounts (IRAs). Today there are some $9.4 trillion dollars invested in IRAs.[9] For an increasingly carbon-conscious public, co-ops must be leaders in carbon reduction while rewarding their members for doing so. As part of an aspirational electric strategy, cooperatives can embrace the Carbon IRA and lead their members through the transition to carbon-free electricity with the necessary urgency. To that, the carbon-backed IRA doesn't answer the question, "Can we do it again?" Rather, it is responsive to a far more important question, "What else can we do for our member-owners?"

Chapter 15

The Cap Rock Way

The history of Cap Rock Electric based in Midland, Texas started in 1939. Its history is a similar story shared by most electric cooperatives to bring the next greatest thing to the surrounding rural areas. According to the history of Cap Rock,[1] the co-op started its Depression era by serving some 2,000 customers. While many co-ops expanded into selling appliances to build load, Cap Rock veered into telephone and formed a cooperative called Cap Rock Refrigeration Cooperative. At the time, that processing co-op was among the nation's most successful slaughtering plant which also processed and stored meat for its members and for "the people in a wide area of west Texas."

You could point to those subsidiary actions as being in the best interests of the members. Decades later, that cooperative spirit would principally enrich one individual. Before that occurred, Cap Rock first yearned, perhaps, to aggrandize its membership. Here's where we learn more about Steve Collier, one of that program's most fascinating and provocative thinkers who, as it turned out, had NBA aspirations.

Collier once set the all-time New Mexico high school record by racking up sixty-nine points wearing the colors of Carlsbad High School. That netted him an appointment from President Nixon to attend West Point where Steve played under Bobby Knight and roomed near General David Petraeus and future astronaut Frank Borman. After a back injury, Steve transferred to New Mexico State where he played under basketball coach Lou Henson. Steve was good enough to be invited to try out for the Houston Rockets which included Elvin Hayes, Rudy Tomjanovich, and Spud Webb and convinced him to take his talents instead to Purdue University. There Steve graduated with a masters degree in electrical engineering. His graduate paper centered on high voltage corona physics.

Later, Steve would work for C. H. Guernsey where he was recruited in 1989 by Cap Rock CEO Dave Pruitt to be Vice President of Government Relations and Power Supply. Collier was tasked to pass a deregulation measure at the Texas capital which was not much liked by the Texas Electric Cooperative. Collier was also featured that same year jumping in the air like Eddie Van Halen on the cover of RE Magazine's issue titled Highfliers.

Co-ops are generally loath to compete with their members. Cap Rock, nonetheless, decided to enter into the oil and gas business. They thought that if 70 percent of the co-op's load harvested the variety of Texas crude, then they had best get to know that business. Once the co-op purchased, of all things, a Detroit company called Detroit Texas Gas Gathering, Cap Rock added an outside director by the name of Donnie Evans. Evans was then the CEO of Tom Brown Oil and Gas, the co-op's largest member. Evans would later be named as Secretary of Commerce under George W. Bush. After their audacious purchase, Cap Rock was captive to its power supplier, Texas Utilities. They decided to build some 300 miles of high-voltage transmission lines that would allow the co-op to access cheaper power from the Southwest Power Pool, saving Cap Rock members a considerable amount of money.[3]

In 1991, Cap Rock purchased Lone Wolf Electric Cooperative, perhaps among the coolest named co-ops ever, and a year later added Hunt-Collins Electric Co-op. Lone Wolf may have been contiguous as its headquarters were but 80 miles away but it's unlikely that Hunt-Collins was since they were located in Greenville, nearly 400 miles away. Later on, Cap Rock attempted to purchase the assets of the Vermont and Hawaii-based Citizens Electric, decidedly out of the Cap Rock service area, which until 2005 would have been illegal for public companies, i.e., IOUs. Here I will pause to give you information on PUHCA.[5]

In 1935, Montana Senator Burton Wheeler and the progenitor of REA, Texan Sam Rayburn, introduced the Public Utility Holding Company Act arguing that the power companies had gone well beyond normal business functions to private socialism. Essentially, according to Wikipedia,[6] the law gave the Securities and Exchange Commission authority to regulate, license, and break up electric utility holding companies. It limited holding company operations to a single state, thus subjecting them to effective state regulation. It also broke up any holding companies with more than two tiers, forcing divestitures so that each became a single integrated system serving a limited geographic area. Another purpose of PUHCA was to keep utility holding companies that were engaged in regulated businesses from also engaging in unregulated businesses. Being a co-op bestowed several celestial attributes, among them not having to adhere to the holding company limitations.

Turning again to the history of Cap Rock,[7] here's what next unfolded. By 1993, Cap Rock supplied power to 25,000 meters in a service area that was similar in size to the state of Maryland. At that time, it had revenues of approximately $40 million. In early 2000, the non-profit Cap Rock Electric Co-op, Inc. was on its way to becoming an investor-owned, for-profit organization called Cap Rock Energy Corp. That was the result of a decision made at the co-op's October 1998 meeting. In early 2000, Cap Rock was serving 34,000 customers in twenty-eight Texas counties.

The decision to become an investor-owned utility coincided almost exactly with when the Texas Legislature initiated electricity market deregulation in 1999. The Wall Street Journal[8] on September 23, 1998 said that co-ops were preparing for deregulation through mergers, buying customers, diversifying into other businesses, developing a brand (i.e., Touchstone Energy), and attempting to protect G&Ts. TEC CEO Mike Williams was quoted saying, "Retail competition would have a ripple effect on these larger groups of co-ops (i.e., G&Ts) which depend on predictable demand from individual co-ops. If customers of individual co-ops sign up with other electricity providers," Williams said, "that brings instability to the G&Ts." Three years later in 2002, consumers who were principally served by IOUs could choose their electric suppliers. Co-ops, unless they chose to do so, were exempt which proved the value of the TEC's legislative representation.[9]

Collier, who both agitated for legislation allowing retail choice and the construction of transmission to access cheaper power, was the go-to guy to deal with Detroit oil interests. Collier left the co-op after disagreements with Pruitt in 1995. Four years later in 1999, Cap Rock Energy, formerly Cap Rock Electric Cooperative, finally achieved legislative success when the Texas legislature allowed the co-op to have, at least for them, the best of two worlds. That was customer choice legislation and a legislative provision allowing Cap Rock to convert from a co-op to a stock company while, but get this, retaining the market protections afforded co-ops according to a 2003 Gismedia web site entry.[10]

A November 21, 2002 Texas for Public Justice Lobby Watch provided even more detail when that publication reported:[11]

"Cap Rock hired lobbyist Christi Craddick in 1999 to make it the only co-op in the state that could convert to an investor-owned utility without losing its co-op perks. Presumptive next House speaker Tom Craddick—who happens to be Christi's dad—inserted the magic words into the deregulation bill. Crediting the Craddick family, internal Cap Rock documents later gloated, 'No one gave us any chance of pulling this off, and we feel we did the impossible.'"

With deregulation, according to a study published by the Texas Coalition for Affordable Power, Texans spent $22 billion dollars more since 2002 compared to that paid by Texans living outside deregulation which included the cooperatives and municipalities. That amounted to more than $4,500 for a typical household from 2002 until the report's 2014 publication. That's not all. According to the March 2014 report, Texans largely located in IOU territory which serves about 85 percent of the population are also on the hook for some $7 billion in assets owned by IOU that became uneconomical, or stranded, under customer choice.[12] Those deregulation costs that were designed, of course, to allow customer choice presumably to lower electric bills would soon be found to be just the opposite.

In March 2002, Cap Rock Energy issued common stock with The American Stock Exchange under the ticker symbol RK. Here's how the membership benefitted according to the Brady Standard Herald article dated March 1, 2002:[13]

- 1,302,355 shares were divided among the 26,634 former members of the co-op.

- All capital credits totaling $26,632,609 were returned to the membership.
- Members were given the option to receive capital credits on a discounted basis, credit on their electric bill, or shares of stock which 69 percent chose to do.

Dave Pruitt, the co-op's then CEO, said, "The number of members choosing to receive stock is a clear mandate to us from former members that they value our vision."[14]

Three years later, a November 2005 press release announced that Cap Rock Energy Corp, once known as Cap Rock Electric, was sold to Lindsay Golberg for $21.75 a share making the sale worth some $163 million. Of note was this acknowledgement: "Certain of the Company's shares which are held by certain members of management will be rolled over into shares of a new parent company controlled by LG. Following the transaction, the Company will no longer have any publicly traded shares."[15]

The management was Cap Rock CEO Dave Pruitt who became a "consultant to the Company, serving as Senior Advisor to the board of directors and management." LG, by the way, describes its business philosophy as, "We've built Lindsay Goldberg with the goal of serving as the absolute best partner for family and founder-led businesses."[16]

If 69 percent of the members chose stock and it was divided equally, which it would not have been based on the size of load, then those choosing stock received 71 shares which is based on 69 percent of the membership choosing to do so. The sale of Cap Rock to LG at $21.75 a share would have netted the average member $1,544. While that might have been a welcome amount, it fell far short of the amount that each of the 26,634 members would have received if they benefitted equally from shares of the $163 million paid which would have been an average of $6,120 per member. Again, that amount would have varied based on the amount of electricity used.

So much for that family-centric company. According to the Dallas Morning News dated December 17, 2009[17] it was reported that Hunt Consolidated Inc.'s electricity unit, Sharyland Utilities, had signed a deal to buy West Texas utility Cap Rock Energy Corp. for $221.5 million, allowing LG to pocket close to $60 million. The deal expanded Sharyland's reach to twenty-eight counties in West and North Texas, including some areas of Collin and Hunt counties. Sharyland gained 38,000 customers.

Hunt Consolidated is the progeny of H. L. Hunt who, according to legend, cashiered his poker winnings to purchase the East Texas oil fields. Forbes Magazine estimated in 1957 that H. L. Hunt was the seventh richest man in the world.[18] Among the fifteen children Hunt sired was Lamar Hunt who founded the American Football League, owned the Kansas City Chiefs, and allegedly coined the term Super Bowl. Perhaps the most notorious Hunt was Nelson Bunker, nicknamed at least in the press as Bunkie. You may recall that Hunt was convicted in 1979 for attempting to corner the silver market.

Sharyland Utilities, once a subsidiary of the Hunt oil and gas conglomerate, is now co-owned by the San Diego-based Sempra Utilities. Sempra Energy says its "mission is to be North America's premier energy infrastructure company." In 2018, Sempra reported revenues of more than $11.6 billion from providing, according to the company's website, to approximately 40 million consumers worldwide.[19]

How did the former member-owners of Cap Rock fare? Not well. Texas Monthly, one of the nation's best publications, reported in 2016[20] that the customers of Sharyland Utilities, once the members of Cap Rock, suffered under the highest rates in the state despite deregulation adopted in Texas allowing IOU customers to choose their energy supplier. What they couldn't select, however, was their wires supplier and Sharyland took full advantage of their ability to charge a 35 percent tax rate to their customers which, in turn, was never paid by Sharyland. It avoided doing so by setting up what is called a REIT or Real Estate Investment Trust, whose investors instead paid taxes on their earnings from the Trust thus absolving Sharyland from that tax burden. The PUC allowed the Trust to pocket that enormous overage and later adopted in 2013 a cost-of-service rate which furthermore penalized the former co-op members whose sparsity led to yet more rate increases reflecting the true cost of serving rural Texas. Had Cap Rock stayed a co-op, their rates would have been substantially less, based on this reporting from the same article:[21]

"And the Office of Public Utility Counsel, a state agency that is tasked with representing ratepayers, is laser-focused on the issue as well. It noted in a filing last year that a handful of rural Texas cooperatives with small customer bases and wide service areas charge half of what Sharyland charges. [Sharyland's] delivery charges are an outlier among both investor-owned utilities and smaller rural electric utilities, the filing said."

Pruitt, presumably happy, did well. Quite well. According to the MRT Insider dated March 20, 2005,[22] here's what the Texas PUC heard when Cap Rock Energy filed for a rate increase:

"A recent hearing has raised questions of poor management and improper executive perks at a West Texas energy utility. According to testimony presented to a panel of three administrative judges last week in Austin, Midland-based Cap Rock Energy Corp. paid for trips to Bermuda, the Caribbean, Arizona, and Colorado for its chief executive officer, David Pruitt and his wife, even though the company was suffering operating losses and looking to increase rates.

Cap Rock also paid for the use of a private jet for other executives and spent more than $16,000 on questionable hotel expenses. Their recommendation now goes to the Texas Public Utility Commission, which is expected to make a final ruling in about two months. According to evidence cited in the case, company officers and directors earned more than $1 million in bonuses between 1996 and 2001 despite operating losses during the same period."

As an IOU, Cap Rock Energy had to file what's called a 10-K report required by the Securities and Exchange Commission that purports to provide a comprehensive summary of a company's financial performance. For co-ops, the 990 report provides similar information including the salaries of management and the board of directors.

The 10-K filed by Cap Rock Energy[23] shows Pruitt's total compensation package through December 31, 2002 as $473,656. He also had 31,788 shares of stock which peaked at $11.65. Beside that largesse, Pruitt's contract extended for ten years with an additional three-year term following the eighth year if no one raised an objection the previous year. Thereafter, Pruitt saw each year add an additional three years unless there was a termination notice ninety days prior to his anniversary date. All that for, as the Texas Monthly described, a tiny utility. But that wasn't the best part.

If there was a change in control, meaning if Cap Rock Energy was sold and Pruitt was terminated, Pruitt would receive an amount six times his salary of $214,995 that would equal $1,289,970. Pruitt's contract, noted in the corporation's 10-K report, would also pay him the "greater of the highest bonus award to him in the previous year or 50 percent of his base salary. Pruitt's bonus at the end of 2002 was $39,000 so it's likely he took the 50 percent salary provision of $107,498 or a multiple of six times his salary for an additional $645,000. In total, the LG buyout netted Pruitt $1,934,955. Perhaps its superfluous to mention that Pruitt also received health care coverage.

Pruitt died in early January 2020. In his obituary, his accomplishments were listed as being all-district in track and football and that he was converting Cap Rock Electric Cooperative to an investor-owned utility, the first co-op to do so. To date, no other co-op has yet to follow.

Chapter 16

1st Rochdale Cooperative

Before the 21st Century Committee inquired whether we could do it again, there was a different question in the late 1990s that asked, "Can we do it?"

That same lament was asked during the height of the depression. Yet groups of farmers assembled to answer in the affirmative with some scratching to get the three consumers per mile necessary to obtain REA loans. Some sixty years later, New Yorkers started asking the same question.[1] Here's what happened according to an article in the October 2001 Cooperator New York, the Co-op and Condo resource[2] which reported that the 1st Rochdale Cooperative Group formed in 1997 was going to entertain electric service to contend with the prospects of skyrocketing energy costs. The allowance by the State of New York to create Energy Service Companies or ESCOs to compete against an incumbent utility, allowed Cooperative Housing to compete against Commonwealth Edison. That's how the 1st Rochdale Cooperative came into being. By way of background, the Rochdale Society of Equitable Pioneers, founded in 1844, was an early consumer cooperative and one of the first to pay a patronage dividend, forming the basis for the modern cooperative movement.[3]

The Cooperator New York article named Allen Thurgood as the 1st Rochdale Board Chair and he received technical assistance from NRECA. Showing an abundance of optimism, Thurgood said the 1.2 million New Yorkers living in housing cooperatives should be afforded the advantages an electric cooperative could provide. The fledging electric cooperative named Greg Wortham, the former NRECA Senior Corporate Counsel, as the Chief Operating Officer for 1st Rochdale.

Thurgood is one of those prominent co-op innovators. He was the Executive Director of the Coordinated Council of Housing Services in New

York, representing an astonishing 1.2 million housing co-op residents. So beloved and respected was Thurgood that he was inducted into the Cooperative Hall of Fame in 2004.[4] According to Wortham, Thurgood was a visionary with extensive New York contacts who literally willed 1st Rochdale into existence. The hall of famer's efforts were similar to a housewife and prison guard in Eastern Oregon who did something similar fifteen years earlier. More on her later.

The idea of an electric cooperative was met with great skepticism, if not ridicule, as reported by Cooperator New York, The Co-op and Condo Resource.[5] Enlisting NRECA seemed to assuage the doubters and including 1st Rochdale as its first urban co-op gave NRECA something they never had which was an urban co-op whose membership potentially included five times the customers as Pedernales Electric based in Texas, then and now the nation's largest electric cooperative.

While NRECA was all set to participate in New York City's customer choice, most statewides representing their co-op members were busy opposing customer choice or retail wheeling as it was also called. The collective lot argued that co-ops that serve far-flung rural areas would be a disadvantage when energy marketing companies targeted the few commercial and industrial customers co-ops served. Nonetheless, here's what NRECA was thinking according to testimony by Greg Wortham, NRECA Senior Corporate Council before the Consumer, Environment and Education Task Force of the Subcommittee Studying Electric Utility Restructuring for The General Assembly Commonwealth of Virginia on September 17, 1998—a year after 1st Rochdale started:[6]

> "1st Rochdale Cooperative Group, Ltd., an aggregation energy services cooperative, was formed in September 1997 by a central organization representing approximately 50,000 New York City families that live in and own housing cooperatives. All told, roughly 500,000 families (about 1.2 million people) in four boroughs of New York City live in and own housing cooperatives. The housing cooperatives range from low income to Park Avenue and Central Park West. These thousands of individual housing cooperatives work together through a small number of coalitions on various issues. These coalitions are seriously

considering joining the 1st Rochdale initiative to purchase electricity and other energy and energy services jointly. Other potential participating groups include the similarly situated high-rise residential buildings (such as condominiums and apartments), commercial high-rise buildings, and public institutions (such as colleges, universities, hospitals, and performing arts centers)."

Wortham would add that the primary goal of 1st Rochdale was to lower its members' energy bills rather than lower electric rates. Doing so, of course, meant providing energy conservation, renewables, contemplating microturbines, and get this, photovoltaics and fuel cells. Pretty heady energy contemplation in 1997, well before solar let alone fuel cells, and would see great prominence.

Forming 1st Rochdale also meant the fledging electric cooperative first had to meet New York state's restructuring rules which include becoming an ESCO or electric service company. Here's how Wortham described the challenge of being an ESCO to the Cooperator Newsletter:[7]

"In the New York market, there are many other providers. But we are having the same problems as other ESCOs in terms of regulatory obstacles and finding ways to communicate electronically. We're looking at other ways to draw the community together. A few years ago, there were 70 to 80 ESCOs now there are only five or six remaining–1st Rochdale is one of them. Many tried to get too big too quickly. We are taking steps to avoid that. We rely on cooperative coalitions, trade shows, networking and word-of-mouth to make our services known. We are working with electric cooperatives with over 60 years' experience as energy providers."

Wortham noted that Housing cooperatives were always served in their entirety. Among the housing cooperatives spread across New York City's five boroughs are Trump Village 3 and 4 built by Fred Trump. Wortham said Fred Trump later spun off those units which kept the name until the day after his son, President Donald Trump, was elected.

"Served in their entirety," begs some explanation. A housing co-op at least until the 1950s was mastered metered, meaning the building's residents split the one bill based on apartment size. During that time, the New York Public Service Commission wanted to prevent a landlord from sticking residents with high bills but that was a bit of a curiosity since the buildings were cooperatives. That remained the practice into the 1980s. In a New York Times article entitled How to Cut Utility Cost in a Co-op,[8] the author talked about potential savings based on energy conservation but allowed that the cost of installing individual meters in the co-op housing apartments could be daunting. To that, the housing co-op trade publication noted as late as 2007 that, "One element that can seriously complicate submetering[9] is if there are rental units in the building and the PSC requires boards to submit detailed information about its submetering plan."

For 1st Rochdale, the fact the housing co-ops served were master metered meant the co-op could grow quickly, almost exponentially, based on the cost of electricity which varied hour by hour. Wortham recalled that on a very hot July day housing co-op members joined 1st Rochdale based on a local radio station saying the new electric co-op could save serious American currency while solving sweltering. Thousands did so and later thousands changed their minds. However, it was the addition of the American Express load that carried the co-op and helped pay for the wheeling costs imposed by the New York ISO. Wortham said American Express issued a request for electric service which 1st Rochdale won "because our aggregated cooperative team worked collaboratively through the July 4 holiday and submitted an effective team response."

1st Rochdale agreed to use the AmEx Corporate Card billing procedure as that was an AmEx requirement that Con Ed solutions refused to use. Wortham said that load was about 3–5 MW. White shoes Wortham, benefitting his interest in tennis, also recalled that 1st Rochdale supplied electricity to the New York National Tennis Center which hosted the US Tennis Open.

As Glenn English recalled in a September 2020 email,[10] other than moral support, NRECA wasn't all that much involved. Wortham, English noted, was the point guy. The formation of 1st Rochdale, the former Oklahoma Congressman said, reminded him of their roots when a group of consumers united to improve their lives and believed it was something that could refresh the electric cooperative movement after what was then sixty years. English, the longest serving NRECA CEO added that:

> "It seemed to me, many in the electric coop program were mouthing the words but acting like IOUs. I hoped we could use these new co-ops, like 1st Rochdale to generate a new wave of consumer power through electric cooperatives. Today, some of that is happening through broadband and individual projects. I believed we could use the local electric cooperative as the community vehicle to meet the needs of the community. For that to work, the local co-op board, manager and staff had to work closely with co-op members. The us against them mentality we see in far too many co-ops made that impossible."[11]

Beside the efforts to reinvigorate the co-op movement, at least in the early 2000s, 1st Rochdale's energy aspirations went far beyond being an electric aggregator. The co-op which adopted "What can we do for you" provided comprehensive energy management supplying not only electrons but oil, gas, and even DirecTV through NRTC.[12] To all that, 1st Rochdale was an active voice in supporting legislation to develop alternative energy sources and address energy-related environmental issues. The group was at the forefront of researching and developing technologies to reduce emissions and clean up traditional power plants, leading to cleaner neighborhoods and a cleaner environment.

Most of NRECA's members were doing just the opposite by opposing renewable mandates and conservation mandates that interfered with the sale of carbon-based electricity because that revenue was needed to pay off burgeoning loans. Within the decade, most statewides were forced to capitulate if not endorse renewable mandates, or at least carve out concessions for co-ops.

1st Rochdale also created the Green Apple Renewable Energy Program,[13] which Wortham said was developed to find alternatives to current energy sources including solar, a technology that would be embraced by most co-ops a decade later. Equally prescient was Green Apple efforts to develop Distributed Generation (DG) technologies. DG can produce electric power near the site where it's needed most, making it particularly useful in remote and non-grid areas. Had it been perfected, it likely would have kept the lights on when Hurricane Sandy left 8 million New Yorkers out of power in late November 2012.[14] Presaging the end of 1st Rochdale was this observation Wortham made to the newsletter:

> "Since its inception, 1st Rochdale has tried to tune in to what most New Yorkers are looking for in an energy provider: quality customer service, fair prices, and a sense of environmental responsibility. Time will tell if this conscientious newcomer has struck upon the right formula for success and longevity in the competitive energy marketplace."

English said this about 1st Rochdale's demise: "The short answer was access to affordable generation and transmission. Commonwealth Edison was politically more powerful than housing co-ops and much of that was linked to money. This effort shows again why so many co-ops built G&Ts, even with very politically powerful co-ops of the 1960s and 1970s.

NRECA Executive Vice President Martin Lowery also observed, "I can say for sure that this was a Hail Mary pass on the possible role of cooperatives in the environment of NY electricity deregulation. In particular, as Wortham affirmed, the churn rate of some 35 percent of the customer base was impossible to deal with for a cooperative that anticipated a stable revenue stream. There was also very negative feedback from the upper Midwest, regarding preference power. I recall at the Region VII meeting (prior to regional consolidation) that a well-respected rancher from Wyoming came to the microphone and strongly argued that we were, inaccurately and with no evidence, jeopardizing WAPA power by supporting 1st Rochdale's potential access to New York Power Authority power."[15]

Five years later in 2003, 1st Rochdale closed its doors. Ed Yakey, a board member and a member of the Housing Cooperative, said the co-op lasted far longer than most ESCOs but the lack of money and the wherewithal to deal with the multiple regulations imposed on ESCOs by the New York Independent System Operator or ISO could only be met by the incumbent IOU, Commonwealth Edison.[16]

Steve Collier—yes, the NBA aspirant—observed that the "complexities of competitive retail power markets and the paucity of public and legislative support doomed this attempt at creating a new cooperative movement with this model. The participants also had very limited financial resources for studies and organization."

Collier added, "It's interesting that a side effect of this at best intellectual skirmish with competitive retail power markets was the birth of ACES which was formed because many G&T CEOs came to the realization that they did not have the scale or expertise to operate in competitive wholesale power markets."

When asked what lessons were learned, Glenn English observed that they knew success was a long shot but there was nothing to lose from NRECA's standpoint. In fact, politically it gave them a chance to emphasize their purpose and talk to elected officials as well as community leaders who knew little or nothing about who they were. Upon reflection, he wondered how much interaction there was between co-op housing leadership and members.

Perhaps more important was this thought that English offered: "NRECA was on the side of the angels in these efforts and we had nothing to lose. I believe in the you grow, or you die approach either as a person or business. I believe electric co-ops should press the envelope seeking ways to improve the lives of the membership and do more to build support. We have mouthed the words 'we were born in politics and if we die, we will die in politics.' Far too often, we forget that political power comes from the membership." Which foretold of cooperative evangelism that would add over half a million new co-op members.

Chapter 17

Co-op Evangelism

I n 1987, California-Pacific National looked to sell its Eastern Oregon territory including the towns of John Day, Baker City, LaGrande, and Burns. Neighboring Idaho Power was the logical choice to take over the nearly 25,000 customers and, indeed, the potato state IOU offered $65 million to do so. That offer was derailed over differences, the most notable being union contracts as reported by the UPI on December 31, 1986: "The International Brotherhood of Electrical Workers filed a complaint with the National Labor Relations Board and a federal lawsuit to block the sale. The union said its contract prohibited any change of ownership that did not recognize the existing labor agreement."[1]

What happened next was extraordinary. Peggi Timm was a self-described housewife and, for a time, a prison guard who hailed from, in her words, the deep South surrounded by cotton but absent electricity. Following the failure of CP National to sell its facilities to Idaho Power, Peggi—a well-known civic leader of Baker City—decided quite by herself that perhaps a cooperative would be better for the now nearly 30,000 customers. Sufficiently convinced, Peggi along with her husband Glenn and Dick Haynes then convinced 700 of their pals and acquaintances to become co-op members for a one cent membership fee. That $7 leveraged a loan from CFC for $24.5 million. While decidedly less than what Potato Power offered, there existed no bank in the FDIC family or otherwise that would loan that amount based on $7 in equity. But that's exactly what CFC did.[2]

In 2013, Peggi Timm passed away.[3] Her funeral attracted a large gathering including two Oregon Governors, Neil Goldschmidt and Ted Kulongoski, attesting to their admiration in the unwavering belief of one woman who created what's now Oregon's largest electric cooperative. And because Peggi was such a transformative person and co-op director, she personified the late Supreme Court Justice Ruth Bader Ginsburg who said, and it should also be the co-ops' calling: "To make life a little better for people less fortunate than you, that's what I think a meaningful life is."[4] That unwavering belief resided in the most unlikely of sources, a bespectacled and voluble Harvard MBA and pilot who expanded the co-op footprint to Hawaii.

Bill Collet got his start assisting co-ops to acquire territory, an ethic Collet and CFC would engineer by adding literally hundreds of thousands of new co-op members. Until then, co-ops fought to hold on to territory from munis who held the long belief of municipal manifest destiny. Before all that happened, however, Collet was invited to assist Cap Rock Electric, based in Texas, to acquire an IOU in June of 1989.

As Collet recalled, Texas Utilities had just won a rate case to put the Comanche Peak nuclear plant, which was five times over budget, into the rate base. Cap Rock, an all-requirements customer of that giant IOU, had a contract clause that allowed Cap Rock to cancel the contract if the rate change exceeded a cap amount which the new nuclear plant triggered. Cap Rock wanted to shop for power supply or maybe build its own gas generation but did not have enough load to really interest alternative suppliers. Collet said he and Cap Rock developed a plan to make a run to acquire taking over a small IOU called Southeastern Electric Service Company (SESCO) based in Jackson, Texas. Like Cap Rock, SESCO was also an all-requirements TXU customer. Purchasing SESCO would have increased the size of the load to expand energy options for Cap Rock. SESCO was small but had been an IOU traded on the NYSE for decades. Collet recalled planning for Cap Rock to acquire a 5 percent stake through market trades which was below the Securities and Exchange Commission reporting limit. They then went to talk to CEO Lyle Goforth who had been running SESCO for years. Cap Rock was able to obtain the 5 percent number which increased the stock to about $44 per share. Goforth had no interest in selling out to the co-op and he immediately got on a plane to Dallas to meet with TXU. About a month later, TXU announced it was buying SESCO for $96 per share in cash. Cap Rock made a $19 million profit on their stake as TXU was sending the message, don't screw with me in Texas. Later on, Cap Rock Electric, of course, became a cautionary tale.

Collet, along with his partner Terry Christenberry would later form Christenberry Collet & Company, Inc. based in Kansas City and they proceeded to get busy assisting co-ops. That included assisting the Alaska-based Matanuska Electric fend off a hostile takeover from Chugach which was both a distribution and a generating and transmitting co-op. Collet also participated in the rescue of the Wolverine Power Cooperative, a G&T based in Cadillac, Michigan which was almost bankrupt because of its ownership in the Fermi II nuclear plant. Fermi II saw the original project cost of the plant pegged at $300 million ending up costing more than a billion dollars before it was finished.[5]

Then came Citizens Utilities which supplied power to Kauai Island and counted some 35,000 customers.[6] In 2001, Citizen's electric rates were 69 percent higher than the neighboring island of Oahu. The utility counted a renewable portfolio of 9 percent, mostly derived from plantation era hydro. The Citizen Utility, bent on selling, conducted an auction where KUIC agreed to $280 million, which the Hawaii Public Utilities Commission rejected as too high. Collet entered the picture and renegotiated a price of $215 million, which was one CFC thought could be financed, and the deal was completed in November 2002. In the ensuing 18 years, KIUC went from zero equity to 34 percent. Rates have declined from 46 cents to 34 cents making KIUC the second cheapest among the six islands and get this: KIUC over the full year of 2020 ran at 100% on its renewable energy sources for over 1,500 hours and achieving some hours of 100% renewable generation almost every day.

From 9 percent renewable in 2001, according to its 2019 annual report KIUC recounted that of the 236 MW needed, more than half or 56 percent came from renewables. Those were mostly solar including that nearly 17 percent of their members had rooftop solar which all told saved islanders some $50 million that the co-op would have otherwise paid for diesel fuel. Of the diesel fuel used, the annual report said that the source of generation was synchronized to firm up the intermittent nature of solar which turned out to be the first of its kind ever. To that, KIUC and Tesla opened both an additional 13 MW solar project and a 52 MWh battery energy storage system with a twenty-year fixed price of 13.9 cents.[7]

Get this, as well: The co-op has returned over $40 million to its members in the form of capital credits and counts a reliability factor well beyond 99.9. That's perhaps the best deal Collet did, but these co-ops might say otherwise:

In 2006, Aquila, which would later be branded as Black Hills Energy, sold the Kansas electric properties to Sunflower Electric, the Kansas-based G&T which then spun off an estimated 48,000 customers to six Kansas co-ops: Lane-Scott Electric Cooperative, Prairie Land Electric Cooperative, Inc., Pioneer Electric Cooperative, Inc., Victory Electric Cooperative Association, Western Cooperative Electric Association, and Wheatland Electric Cooperative.

Valley Electric based in Pahrump, Nevada decided to invest in fiber for the homes of its 17,500 members in 2017. The cost to do so soared to some $100 million. Here's some perspective. Collet notes that it cost about $5,500 in distribution and generation costs to serve a single customer which, based on monthly electric usage, is a manageable debt. Fiber, by comparison, costs about $9,000 per customer, and not every customer will pay the freight in order to download dogs riding on skateboards. Collet, called to get the co-op back in the black, engineered a sale of the co-op's high voltage transmission lines which fortuitously was part of the California Independent System Operation. Collet said those assets had a book value of $82 million but an auction fetched an astonishing $200 million from GridLiance. That payment was sufficient to retire the co-op's transmission debt to CFC, pay off the fiber bill, and keep the co-op out of bankruptcy court.[8] Which turned out to be an equitable outcome for those Nevadans.

What Collet did for Cloverland Electric, a Michigan-based electric co-op, made him the co-op's acquisitive version of Samuel Insull. Here's how their website describes the co-op: "Cloverland Electric Cooperative was founded in 1938 to provide electricity across the rural communities of Michigan's Eastern Upper Peninsula. The co-op acquired Edison Sault Electric in 2010, nearly doubling the size of Cloverland's member base. Cloverland Electric started with 1,090 members and now powers over 33,000 members across five counties."

Its Collet's deal with Edison Sault Electric, it turned out you can buy love. Edison Sault Electric owned a 36 MW hydro unit located on the Soo Locks which was operated and maintained by the United States Army Corps of Engineers. The locks enable ships to travel between Lake Superior and the lower Great Lakes. Beside the Soo Locks, the IOU served some 23,000 customers, mostly with its 1.1 cent hydro-based rates. To that, Edison Sault Electric owned transmission lines which electrically connected Michigan's upper and lower peninsulas. Edison Sault Electric would later sell out to Wisconsin Electric in 1997. In 2016, nearly fifteen years later, Collet negotiated the sale for $65 million of Edison Sault Electric which is now Wisconsin Electric. The 23,000 customers went to Cloverland which had previously counted 19,500 customers. To that, Cloverland also landed the hydro unit meaning, in Collet's words, that the co-op either got 23,000 customers for free or the hydro generation for the same price.

Any co-op aspiring to answer the 21st Century Committee's question of can we do it again needs a Bill Collet. Here's more proof for that supposition:

> The Minnesota co-op community had long aspired to acquire the Iowa-based Alliant Energy-based Minnesota customers, and a change in leadership at Alliant Energy allowed for a new effort to begin in earnest in 2014. Several factors were in the co-ops' favor including Alliant's long-standing adverse relationship with the Minnesota PUC. In addition, the twelve Southern Minnesota co-ops that were anxious to add 44,000 Alliant customers to the co-op rolls had two of the smartest co-op guys on their side. One was Hap LeVander, a Harvard law graduate, son of Minnesota Governor Harold LeVander, and counsel to Minnesota's two largest cooperatives as well as the Minnesota Rural Electric Association. The other was Bill Collet. Collet reported the purchase price was about 1.4 book or $127 million financed, of course, by CFC. The twelve co-ops formed the Southern Minnesota Energy Cooperative as the financing vehicle and then determined who got what. Collet said the distribution was done on what the economics brought to each co-op and that only got done because of the strong co-op philosophy of the representation of the dozen co-ops. The deal

became final in mid 2015 after LeVander handled all the attendant PUC issues and Collet handled the finances.

There's one more Collet story that needs telling, It is about nuclear power investments that once promised uranium-based power would be too cheap to meter. We'll deal with that before talking about Vermont Electric's investment that entered into bankruptcy due to the co-op's investment in the Seabrook nuclear plant. That particular plant was beset with design and safety flaws. Seabrook was also hampered by the Three Mile Island partial melt down which added credence to the China Syndrome[9] released around the same time and flayed by protestors and Jackson Browne's No Nukes album.[10] That shows yet again the inadvisability of signing onto long-term contracts where a co-op's ability to challenge decisions is hampered by the controlling unit—IOUs and the government. Here's a somewhat quick recitation of co-ops and the atom:

In the 1960s, the Atomic Energy Commission, an agency you likely know as the Nuclear Regulatory Commission,[11] promoted nuclear units to demonstrate the peacetime use of nuclear power. Two G&Ts participated.[12] One was the United Power Association located in Elk River, Minnesota which decided against owning the plant after construction and subsequent operation. The other G&T was Dairyland Power Cooperative based in LaCrosse, Wisconsin. Lacrosse is also the home of the G. Heileman's brewery. Instead of calling the demonstration plant Old Style, Dairyland chose the moniker LaCrosse Area Boiling Water Reactor (LACBWR) in 1973. Dairyland paid a buck for the reactor and the spent fuel which Dairyland and, frankly. most co-ops believed would be reprocessed at the Clinch River Breeder Reactor. In fact, many co-ops kicked over a few bucks annually to fund Clinch River. Had that happened, DPC could have sold that spent fuel for $6 million. That all ended with, dare we say Jimmy Carter, the architect of the 1976 Fuel Use Act. Carter was an opponent of Clinch River because it would produce plutonium, an element much liked by terrorist countries. Carter also alleged that the plant would use technically obsolete technology. While President Reagan was a supporter, the US Senate terminated the project in 1983.[13] Dairyland would pay out over $100 million to store the waste for eighteen years according to an article in the July 9, 2015 LaCrosse Tribune.[14]

In 1971, a supposition based on long-term energy prediction figured the power used by northwest consumer-owned utilities that received all the good stuff from the Bonneville Power Administration would double within the decade. BPA's hydroelectric system simply would not be able to meet that demand. The Washington Public Power Supply System (WPPSS) was started in the 1950s as a means to guarantee electric power to homes and industry in the northwest.[15] Starting in 1977, WPPSS proposed to build five nuclear plants to meet that amped demand. Thinking, perhaps, how hard can this be, the directors and managers soon discovered that building a nuke was actually rocket science stuff. Soon enough, the cost overruns eventually led to what was then the largest default of municipal bonds that were floated to pay for the plants totaling $2.25 billion or $12,000 per customer.[16] The co-ops were let off the hook because the court essentially ruled that affected co-ops didn't know what they were doing. As an aside, perhaps apocryphal, co-ops knew enough not to tell Federated Insurance, whose policies included coverage for nuclear defaults, but they were not smart enough not to include in their deliberative minutes that perhaps they shouldn't tell Federated about that. Then ensued a lawsuit Federated filed against co-ops in Oregon, Washington, Idaho, and parts of Montana. Coffee mugs with Federated logos wouldn't grace co-op CEO desks for years. Federated and northwest electric co-ops are, by the way, great friends these days thanks to the efforts of now retired Federated CEO Frank Fraas and "we can cover that except for nuclear" intoned by current Federated CEO Phil Irwin.

The cost to build two nuclear reactions at Seabrook was expected to cost around $1 billion in 1966 for unit 1.[17] The actual cost was closer to $13 billion or thirteen Minnesota Viking stadiums none which will likely ever see the Vikings play a Super Bowl game in them. Unit 2 never ran and the plant sold off its parts as sort of a nuclear NAPA auto parts store. Which brings us back to Vermont Electric, soon to be suffocated by Seabrook, or so many thought, as told by the New York Times[18] in 1986:

- To try to pay for its nuclear commitments, the co-op has raised its rates 40 percent in less than a year. But even that leaves income too low to cover obligations, and the co-op has been in default since March 31, 1986.

- With seemingly limitless access to credit from the electrification agency, and at interest rates of 5 to 10 percent and sometimes lower, the co-op bought entitlements to power from reactors that totaled 43 megawatts, nearly one-fourth more than it now uses on a peak day. The idea was apparently to resell some of the power at a profit.

- "You have a rural co-op whose debts far exceed the ability to pay, with any kind of conventional ratemaking," said V. Louise McCarren, chairman of the Public Service Board, which has final authority over rates. She estimated that rates would have to rise to triple or quadruple those of neighboring utilities for the co-op to pay its debts.

- In Washington, Harold V. Hunter, Administrator of the Rural Electrification Administration, said bankruptcy was not the answer. "Thank goodness there's a real strong aversion, particularly among some rural people, and the American people, to the word bankruptcy," he said. "I don't think people want to walk away from their debt." But Mr. Starr said that a neighboring farm had gone bankrupt three times in the last six years and that he would prefer the co-op's bankruptcy to his own. He said he now pays more than 10 cents a kilowatt-hour on the 3,000 kilowatt-hours it takes to run his barn each month, while farmers nearby served by private companies pay 5 cents.

How the co-op survived is yet a different story but what happened next in the early 2000s should cement Collet's legend which, in actuality, should be far more storied than it is. The survival involves Citizen's Utilities, the same IOU that earlier was transformed into Kauai Island Utility Cooperative.

In Collet's telling, he again approached Citizens, now called Citizens Communications Company, to inquire about their 21,000 customers that they served in Vermont. Cap Rock CEO Dave Pruitt also attempted to woo Citizens. Collet was far more successful and had engaged in similar negotiations to purchase Citizens assets in Kauai, resulting in a purchase price of $25 million for those customers. The new Citizens transaction more than doubled the size of Vermont Electric. Today, VEC is one of Standard and Poor's highest-rated co-ops, an incredible achievement considering the co-op saw the bright lights that generally herald death.

All told, Collet added some 500,000 astonishing customers to the co-op rolls and would easily place that co-op which, by all rights, should be called the BC Electric Co-op, a bit snappier than WM Collet Electric Cooperative, as one of the largest co-ops in the nation. We've deified great co-op leaders, many who are in the Cooperative Hall of Fame, and those legendary names should include Bill Collet. Those people were heralded in the twentieth century and whose vision, passion, and contributions make co-ops the utilities of choice now in the second decade of the twenty-first century.

Chapter 18

Musing Mergers

The US Energy Information Administration reports that there are 168 investor-owned utilities serving an average of 654,600 electric customers. The two largest IOUs are in California: Pacific Gas and Electric with 5.48 million customers and Southern California Edison Company with 5.07 million customers. In total, those private power companies serve nearly three quarters of the American population.[1]

Electric cooperatives, by comparison, reach out to about 11 percent of the nation's electric populace. What they lack in customers, they more than make up for in the sheer number of co-ops. Again, the US EIA counts 812 co-ops with an average of 24,500 electricity customers each. The largest co-op is Pedernales Electric Co-op in Johnson City, Texas with 333,809 customers, nearly 50 percent more customers than the second-largest co-op, Jackson Electric Member Corporation in Jefferson, Georgia.[2]

The Dakotas, Nebraska, and wide swaths of nowhere average less than two consumers per mile. Many of those electric co-ops, and there are a great many of them, have at best 2,000–5,000 customers. Some of them have more board members than they do employees.

In the late 1990s, the Minnesota Rural Electric Association asked investment banker Bill Collet to group Minnesota's forty-four electric cooperatives into super co-ops. That exercise showed six co-ops average around 200,000 members each. A gathering of co-op managers glowered at the report, noting that the economies of scale weren't "all that great" and that the Statewide's time would be better spent on, well, something else.

Co-op mergers are rare although hybrid mergers sharing CEOs are not. In Minnesota, ten co-ops shared managers as a sop to the irrefutable observation that mergers eliminate duplicative staff. Other co-ops, the ones serving the far reaches of RFD, were of the mind that no one wanted them and, truth be told, that likely was the case. The cost of servicing wide-open spaces is spendy. Xcel Energy, which covers eight states and serves some 3.6 million customers, inquired if co-ops could handle storm-related outages in western Minnesota given the cost of maintaining those sparse accounts.

The also immutable law of economies of scale was likely one reason why Jim Cooper, in his multi-faceted diatribe against co-op operation, asked out loud why there were so many co-ops including his home state of Tennessee tally of twenty-three co-ops. It should be noted that Cooper's Congressional district did not include any co-ops which perhaps explained his bravery on that particular subject.[3]

There is, of course, no doubt that plying rural families with the good stuff, or as the 21st Century Co-op Committee intoned, "Caring about the member," is particularly expensive. Co-ops, as noted, own and operate more miles of line that those 168 IOUs and the nearly 2,000 municipal-owned utilities.[4] Those poles and wires cost a great deal of money and responding to hooligans tiring of shooting up stop signs and training their sights on insulators oftentimes requires cross-county trips to shore up the sagging lines. Distance? Rio Grande Electric Cooperative based in Brackettville, Texas covers 35,000 miles of service territory.[5] It takes two days to drive the co-op's service area, necessitating two annual meetings to account for the distance that members would have to travel to get the calendar giveaway. That's the reason REA was formed—to provide low-interest loans and to provide a kWh for the truly needy that no one else would serve.

Still, when you have two co-ops in the same town, as is true with Blachly-Lane and Lane Electric which serve around Eugene, Oregon, you might wonder why those two co-ops haven't merged. They've studied doing so and the only result was getting a manager fired, board members replaced, and an attitude of "hell no" which is why there remain two co-ops in the same town.

True, there are different board philosophies which are more about board personalities and which could be overcome for the good of the members but too often fall on what's good for the directors. Little wonder NRECA doesn't feature seminars on why co-ops should merge. If a co-op is so inclined, and on occasion economies of scale are so dramatic it really needs to do so, then

CFC shows the numbers documenting enormous savings. NRECA then can facilitate differences between the two different boards. NRECA did note, however, that mergers among the co-ops that are uneconomically small could save customers at least $220 each per year, resulting in huge savings for customers in total. That amount is roughly the equivalent of two free months of electricity.[6]

Take Tri-County Electric based in Rushford, Minnesota and Hawkeye REC sitting in Cresco, Iowa. The two co-ops had long shared a CEO, and a good one, by the name of Brian Krambeer. The rationale of death-do-us-part was summarized in the 2016 annual report which made this observation: "two cooperative boards of directors and two management teams looking to the future to create a sustainable electric cooperative." That's likely the reason but it took an artful CEO to make it happen. As a result, the new co-op called MiEnergy now offers EV charging, solar, and broadband (in concert with Mabel Cooperative Telephone and Spring Grove Communications Cooperative to create MiBroadband). The combined co-op, now numbering over 20,000 members, provided close to $10 million in economic development loans and grants, proving in this case and likely others that the sum is greater than the parts.

Much earlier, Sioux Valley Energy, then and now the largest co-op in South Dakota, and the much smaller neighboring Minnesota co-op called SW Minnesota Electric, merged in 1995. The CEO of the merged co-op which remained Sioux Valley Energy was Jim Kiley. When asked how SVE was able to accommodate the merged board now numbering a dozen, Kiley memorably said, "Our board room is large enough to sleep twelve." These many years later, that observation remains hilarious, but the merger paid off with the SW Minnesota Electric members having access to more services and products than they would have been able to have.

Therein lies another point. Mergers are said to offer economies of scale that eliminates some duplication but they offer something even more important, opportunities. Small co-ops simply do not have the wherewithal to accommodate services and products their members need. Larger co-ops do and they do.

Perhaps the bigger question is why electric cooperatives don't collaborate more with their telephone counterparts. The Montana Electric Cooperative

Association at one time represented the interests of that state's telcos. NRTC had both electric and telephone cooperatives that offered DirecTV to their respective memberships. The NRTC board also included both electric and telephone co-op board members. The culture of the two cooperatives somehow never meshed causing one, if not both, of the co-op entities to think they could do better than the other which unfortunately manifested itself in the mid-1990s.

In 1996, Congress passed the Telecommunications Act[7] which, among other things, established competitive local exchange carriers or CLEX. Essentially, a CLEX is a telephone company that competes with the already established local telephone business by providing its own network and switching. In Minnesota, a number of co-ops started or participated in a CLEX thinking, perhaps, how hard can this be if the local teleco can do it? Pretty hard, as all those co-ops lost their collective asses and racked up huge losses. Not to be outdone, telcos decided to enter into the solar market offering panels to their members who likely wondered what does a communications company know about energy?

The fact of the matter is the electric and telephone co-ops needed each other. Electrics required fiber to talk to substations and to facilitate the smart grid. Their telephone counterparts could have used the billing service offered by the electrics. Telephone co-ops under the leadership of the National Telecommunication Cooperative Association or NTCA[8] were early leaders in smart phones which can be used by consumers to control electric loads and thus lower their electric rates. Far more important is the knowledge and understanding telephone co-ops have about extending broadband, an area in which the electrics had an understanding deficit although they had the capability to place fiber underground or attached to their miles and miles of distribution poles in addition to the wherewithal to market that service.

Happily, that has occurred. Ken Johnson, the former CEO of Co-Mo Electric and for a brief time RUS Administrator, teamed up with neighboring co-ops and a local telephone co-op subsidiary called Kingdom Technology Solutions to offer broadband to that swatch of Missouri.[9] Broadband Communications Magazine noted in a 2017 edition that: "Arrowhead Electric Cooperative in Lutsen, Minnesota built a fiber-to-the-home network and then contracted with Consolidated Telephone Cooperative to deliver services and provide technical support.[10] And the Johnson County Rural Electric Membership Corporation in Franklin, Indiana built its fiber-to-the-home or FTTH network as a joint venture with NineStar Connect, which is both a telephone co-op and an electric co-op, based on the fiber backbone that Johnson County REMC built to connect its substations." Former RUS Administrator Hilda Legg, writing for Broadband Communications, nailed it with this observation:[11]

"Indeed, partnerships between small rural telcos and electric cooperatives are uniquely positioned to succeed where others have failed in reaching wide swaths of the rural United States. Electric co-ops are well-known, established and focused on delivering services to rural consumers in many communities that lack broadband. Small telcos share the same rural roots along with track records of technological innovation and success in rural broadband. Tackling something as complex and challenging as rural broadband calls for an organization that has a proven track record rather than a startup or a company with experience only in settled markets.

Of course, a partnership won't work in every case, and each possible partnership could look different based upon the needs and capabilities of the parties involved – but knowing the electric cooperatives and the rural telcos as well as I do from years of working with both, I see their respective strengths and the significant promise in such opportunities. If these two groups working together and sharing a rural commitment can't get it done, I don't know who can or will!"

Chapter 19

Call Sheldon

When PKM, a northern Minnesota co-op, was flattened by some ice storm or the Red River backing up again, the question was posed to then PKM Manager Chuck Riesen on what he planned to do. "Call Sheldon."

That seems to be the usual case when co-ops found themselves needing cash for something or other or in a bit of trouble. Which the Minnesota Statewide found themselves when Northern Electric Cooperative Association tried to sell out to Minnesota Power in the early 1990s. MP's rates were 80 percent less than the co-op's and yet CFC twice kicked over integrity fund dollars to keep NECA a co-op. Petersen, who is synonymous with CFC, saved 40,000 members in one state because of the integrity fund conceived by Chuck Gill and another great co-op stalwart, Gary Gordy, who handled CFC's external affairs. That program Petersen minded likely rescued several hundreds of thousands cooperative souls among the bank's appreciative borrowers.

Here's Sheldon Petersen's particulars. He started as a staff assistant at the Iowa-based Nishnabotna Electric in 1976. The board of Rock County Electric selected Sheldon as Manager of the Janesville, Wisconsin co-op in 1980 before he joined CFC as a Regional Vice President.

Here's another pause. CFC prefers to tap co-op CEOs for both their managerial and co-op finance acumen as regional vice presidents. That's not always the case as CFC saw the Minnesota Statewide Director of Education Alison Deelstra as a unique talent and pursued her to teach the particulars of finance to co-ops in Minnesota and North Dakota. Petersen's territory in 1983 included Minnesota and parts of surrounding states.

In 1990, Petersen moved to CFC's headquarters then located in Georgetown. Soon after that, CFC left that trendy neighborhood for a high-rise in Herndon,

Virginia near the Dulles airport. There Sheldon did policy, credit, and audit work before then CFC Governor Chuck Gill tapped him as Assistant to the President. Following Chuck's retirement, Sheldon became the CEO and Governor which was an honorific title for financial officers in 1995

Call Sheldon? We did so. Here's what the long-tenured CFC Governor and CEO, who recently was rewarded with a twenty-five-year employment pin as the CEO, with thirty-seven years overall, had to say about where co-ops stand in regard to the 21st Century co-op inquiry. We asked Petersen about co-ops doing it again and worries, missed opportunities, proudest moments, and the reason why he decided to travel to the South Central public power district located in Palisades, Nebraska whose population density is essentially zero. Petersen's responses were all imbued with the unwavering optimism that has buoyed the program and why "call Sheldon" is the antidote to any number of concerns confronting co-ops.

Petersen clearly said co-ops are indeed doing it again, particularly with their role in both managing the COVID 19 crisis and ensuring their members, many who are unable to pay, still are being given light. In particular, Sheldon observed that co-ops, generally, are sticking to their mission to serve the members which becomes paramount as nearly every co-op not only responds quickly and affirmatively to natural disasters but trucks from co-ops are seen across the state and, on occasion, the nation as they come to offer their assistance. The offering of broadband that is aspired to by, say, 20 percent of CFC members, affirms the co-ops' mission to improve quality of life. It is because of the economics that some members are not interested in broadband.

The adage that "The main thing is to keep the main thing the main thing,"[1] prompted Petersen whose surname, it should be noted, is the preferred spelling among the Iowa bowling elite, listed these main things:

1.   Several years ago, CFC saw a need to assist co-ops to do strategic planning. Since doing so, CFC has facilitated over 500 deep thinking sessions for its members which has provided a colossus of data that tell co-ops what their members want. Knowing that and assisted by the Key Ratio Trend Analysis which literally tracks well over 100 determinants and ranking, gives the co-ops

a sizable platform of issues to discuss with their membership. Communicating, Petersen said, and not for the first time, is paramount for co-ops.

2. Cooperative principle #7 on that particular hit parade is all about contributions to the community. Petersen said co-ops have done quite well meeting that particular commandment. Evidence of that opinion could have had Petersen citing the Rural Development Loan and Grant Program or REDLG which has invested millions of dollars in co-op communities.

3. Petersen noted the delivery platform of delivering electricity, solidified by the all-requirement contract, is changing and particularly with the rise of distributed generation if not pursued by competitors like LEAN and Community Choice Aggregators. Petersen said co-ops need to continue emphasizing delivery of renewable energy to their members and begin to think about 100 percent carbon-free amps and how to handle the power intermittency that could confront their members.

4. Earlier we cited Petersen's address at the CFC Financial forum on social responsibility. CFC recently issued a $400 million ESG or environmental social corporate governance bond. Sheldon said, with a measure of disbelief, that the bond was oversubscribed by banks, mutual funds, and investors. That overwhelming investment prompted an interest rate of 1.3 percent on a ten-year bond. That rate is lower than anything similar issued by IOUs. Petersen said the proceeds would assist co-ops in providing broadband and acquiring renewable energy. More to the point is the necessity, Petersen added, that the co-op membership believe strongly in values. Pursuing those values—be they carbon reduction, broadband, or job creation—is an ethic co-ops need to follow with communication of the manifestation of those values to their membership, referring to point 1.

Petersen, while navigating that Wisconsin co-op heard repeatedly, as co-ops did as late as the 1980s, that anything beyond the meter wasn't a co-op concern. Today, Petersen observes that anything beyond the meter presents an opportunity. If, for example, a member wants solar panels on their roofs, they should first turn to what should be their trusted energy provider, the co-op. That, of course, means co-ops need to continue maintaining their edge on technology changes. Petersen was highly complementary of the G&Ts and regulatory and legislative changes and proposals, a province where NRECA and the Statewides have done quite well.

An earlier chapter recalled that CFC, along with NRECA's emphasis on governance, was directed largely by the Governance Task Force created by both co-op institutions. The ensuring eighty-page document issued in 2017[2] can be summarized, Petersen said, by transparency. If the co-op is clear about issues important to the members they have identified, then everything else governance-related falls in line.

If you've thought of people who would make great dinner conversationalists and who would pick up the tab, then Petersen would be that guy and the one making the restaurant reservations. Musing about the FOMO, which hipsters know stands for Fear of Missing Out, Petersen observed that anything CFC may missed out on is not likely because that means the membership did as well. What's important about FOMO, Petersen noted, is not what's whiffed but where or not it fits with the co-ops 'mission. Sheldon ruminated about a Northwest Airline Magazine, yet another Fortune 500 company that is gone, that years ago featured an ad that stated, "Never stop asking why." That, Petersen said, is not only a sign on his bookcase next to a photo of the family, but includes the critical question asking, "Does it matter to the membership?" "You ask that question," the quizzical Peterson intoned, "you won't miss out on much."

The mission of The National Rural Utilities Cooperative Finance Corp. is, "Supporting America's Electric Cooperative Network." Expanding that network is equally relevant and an earlier chapter entitled Cooperative Evangelism talked about CFC and Bill Collet's incredible efforts to form the Kauai Island Utility Cooperative which included convincing a skeptical Hawaii PUC, let alone Citizens Utility and regulators, about the benefits of an electric cooperative and what exactly is a capital credit. They did so and Petersen ranked that among his favorite successes. All told, between Petersen and Collet the co-op community added over 500,000 customers largely served by IOUs which also padded the dues charged by appreciative Statewide. Being a banker, Petersen takes great pride in CFC's market access and so do nearly 345 co-ops who either rely exclusively on CFC for financing or lean to doing so. Sheldon says he calls every CEO of a 100 percent CFC borrower to listen to their concerns and to add, "CFC will make sure your financing is the least of your concerns." With other banks, co-ops have to hire law firms to type out all the loan covenants. CFC does that in house which is why the now retired PKM Manager Chuck Riesen said, "I'm calling Sheldon to help this co-op out."

You may recall an earlier chapter detailing efforts by some members of Tri-State to break their all-requirement contract in favor of a new suitor. Petersen, highly complementary of the G&Ts, said the all-requirement contract represents a critical insurance policy that delivers daily the electricity needed by each and every co-op member. Recall the days of yesteryear when IOUs ditched the co-ops because there was insufficient current to meet the co-ops' growing loads. In response, co-ops created a G&T to meet their power demands. While G&T members are clamoring for more renewables, Petersen again noted that G&Ts provide economies of scale which distribution co-ops largely cannot do. Tri-State's Duane Highley's efforts to create a renewable pool of resources to fund up to 50 percent of the pristine electrons their members might want demonstrates how well G&Ts have responded not only to market demands but to what their distribution co-ops need.

Citing outstanding co-op CEOs is a question Petersen dodged but he did allow how utterly impressed he was with Dale Haugen, Manager of Mountrail-Williams, a North Dakota co-op whose load exploded with the discovering of oil in the Bakken reserve. Petersen recounted visiting that co-op which at one time enlisted over 300 contract linemen to serve the exponential growth of oil wells. Attending to that massive infrastructure, while protecting the existing membership base from unwanted and unwarranted cost, was an incredible undertaking and Petersen recounted with awe at how well Haugen did so.

CFC has a staff of engineers and rate analysts who do cost-of-service studies for CFC members. Doing so, of course, meets a need many smaller distribution co-ops need but would like to avoid the expense. Those studies also tell CFC the needs of their co-ops, allowing them to expand loan portfolios that they might not otherwise have contemplated in addition to developing new services for co-ops to contemplate. That, Petersen noted again, is why CFC issued the ESG or Environmental Social Corporate (and Cooperative) Governance bond to assist in both funding broadband and renewable energy needed by participating co-ops.

Despite its "there's more where that came from" reputation, CFC at times will say no as they did to a co-op that asked for financing to extend fiber optics for high-speed broadband throughout their service area. Another bank provided financing and the results didn't result in anyone's promotion. While that counsel was disregarded, Petersen said CFC first does a risk analysis for a co-op contemplating broadband. Unlike unserved electric needs, competitors have likely taken the best broadband customers while leaving the RFD mailboxes to the co-op. Financing those residential dregs is doable but CFC lending will be done in stages to ensure each step is measured and is able to pay for the capital outlay. As Collet noted, the cost to serve prospective broadband customers exceeds the capital to provide electricity which is why federal loans and grants are necessary. Petersen's thinking, which makes him a cooperative constitutional contextualist, is that CFC knows we will be living with these financial decisions for years to come. Or, better said, our members are us.

Dinner, sadly, was almost over with Sheldon but not before asking him who were among his favorite speakers who addressed the CFC Financial Forums over the years. Here's who he would like to include at his dinner table:

1. Jim Collins, renowned business author whose book, *Good To Great*, is the bestselling business book of all time. Petersen said Collins wouldn't sign a speaking contract with CFC until he fully understood how co-ops work.

2. Former Secretary of State Condoleezza Rice, who Petersen said was one of the most uplifting speakers CFC ever had. After a Rice presentation, you felt you could take on the world.

3. Steve Forbes, past presidential candidate, publisher of Forbes Magazine, and owner of a yacht called The Capitalist Tool. "Forbes," Petersen said, "was incredibly down-to-earth and his views were amazingly practical. One of my favorite guys," he added.

4. Hall of Fame shortstop Cal Ripken, the iron man who played his entire twenty-one seasons with the Baltimore Orioles and who holds the record for consecutive games played at 2,632—breaking Lou Gehrig's streak by over 500 games.

5. Oregon Rural Electric Association Executive Director Theodore Case with the overview of his two books, 1) Power Plays: The U.S. Presidency, Electric Cooperatives, and the Transformation of Rural America; and 2) Poles, Wires and the War: The Remarkable Untold Story of Rural Electrification and the Vietnam War. Petersen said that not only did Ted thrill the audience with an overview of both books but that he was one of CFC's favorites to moderate panels on diverse political views.

6. Former Federal Reserve Chairman Paul Volker, if for no other reason than his courage to raise interest rates to arrest runaway inflation, "even though Volker was somewhat responsible for the interest rate of 15.3 percent on my home in Minneapolis while I was a CFC Regional Vice President."

No interview is complete, at least this one, without asking Sheldon what advice he might have for his successor. Keeping up with technology and regulatory changes is an inevitable suggestion but his observation that traveling to meet the members, while important to remind the membership of the value of CFC, was more telling about Petersen. Here's what he said: "My travel is where I gained intelligence and am reminded of the uniqueness of the electric cooperative culture." Even at the Palisades, Nebraska-based South Central Public Power District.

On a final personal note, upon retiring MREA hosted a reception at a local Maple Grove hostelry on a cold, icy, miserable December day that dissuaded the dissuadable from attending. Sheldon was there. Which, come to think of it, is the near perfect way to describe his stewardship.

Chapter 20

Ask the Chairman

Craig Thomas was the US Senator representing Wyoming from 1994 to 2006.[1] Prior to representing the forty-seventh state, Thomas was the Executive Director of the Wyoming Rural Electric Association. Saxby Chambliss, representing Georgia in the Senate from 2013 to 2015[2] was counsel to several Georgia co-ops as was true with Minnesota Senator Dave Durenberger (1978–1995)[3] and Governor Harold Levander (1967–1971)[4] whose clients included the Minnesota Rural Electric Association. To all that, co-op directors and CEOs have populated state legislatures across the nation. None, however, have ever ascended to chair the Federal Energy Regulatory Commission or FERC as is true with Neil Chatterjee.

After graduation from the University of Cincinnati law school, Neil Chatterjee was a staff member on the House Ways and Means Committee which, among other things, engages in tax policy. From there, Neil was on the staff of Ohio Congresswoman Debra Pryce before being wooed by NRECA where he was handed the captive shipper issue.

Back in the day, and this would be in 1976 when West Virginia Congressman Harley Staggers[5] convinced his colleagues to enact a measure to deregulate the rail industry that was threatened, or so it seemed, by the trucking industry. The Staggers Act allowed more flexibility in pricing but, more important for many G&Ts, the Act permitted acquisition to the point where sixty some different railroads with such lyrical names as The Santa Fe were swept up into seven Class 1 carriers—Union Pacific, Burlington Northern, Canadian Pacific, Canadian National, Norfolk Southern Railroad, Kansas City Southern, and CSX. Captive then meant a host of G&Ts from Basin Electric to Seminole Electric were served by only one railroad which could charge rates up to what it would cost to build a mythical competing railroad. Prices soared.

We'll get back to Neil shortly but here's yet another manifestation of the impact of the 1976 Power Plant Industrial Fuel Use Act. Instead of using natural gas, then captive to the concept of peak gas, G&Ts were served up a heaping of coal whose impacts continue to beguile the industry. The Staggers Act also prompted an organization called CURE which stood for Consumers United for Rail Equity. That effort prompted any number of congressional receptions designed to entice House and Senate members to hear the confiscatory prices charged by railroads but they were generally only attended by interns looking to load up their backpacks with those little smokies. That was the assignment handed to Neil.

Neil did as well as he could before accepting an offer from Senate Majority Leader Mitch McConnell to do the Kentuckian's energy work, particularly important to a state where coal long dominated. McConnell would latter elevate Chatterjee as his chief floor staffer to coordinate the Senate Republicans on legislative matters. Neil did so and did it well for eight years. Shortly after the 2016 election, Chatterjee was confirmed by the US Senate as a Commissioner on the five member FERC body. In 2018, President Trump tapped Chatterjee as the Commission's Chair.

Before commencing with the Chatterjee chitchat, perhaps you're curious about the genesis of FERC. Here we cover a century of energy policy history quite quickly.

In 1920, Congress first entered into the shallow pool of electric regulation when it enacted the Federal Water Power Act centering on hydroelectricity. Fifteen years later, FDR was frustrated by the successful efforts of IOUs to skip any sort of oversight and he introduced in 1935 Part II of the Federal Power Act (FPA), attempting to address energy market dominance[6]. In yet another Jimmy Carter effort to make the then energy crisis the equivalent of war, Congress in 1977 created the Federal Energy Regulatory Commission (FERC). The agency's initial jurisdiction was over the wholesale energy market. Next FERC minded transmission rates and where those towers could be plunked down to create a regional transmission organization or RTO which then segued to pricing electricity sales[7] to, well, we'll get to that in a bit.

We caught up with Chatterjee shortly after he issued a policy statement (Docket No. AD20-14-OOO) "clarifying that FERC has jurisdiction over organized wholesale electric market rules that incorporate a state-determined carbon price in those markets.[8]

Whew.

In the span of four short years, carbon emissions wafting from power plants were said to contribute to climate change, were regarded as a hoax by the Trump Administration, and then were regarded as a traceable commodity. Carbon emissions, in essence, would be priced in the same fashion as electrons are valued by regional transmission organizations. After Chatterjee issued that policy and then chatted it up, the White House Office of Personnel removed him as Chair of FERC two days after the 2020 election.[9] The demotion didn't faze Chatterjee. During a conversation, the then deposed Chairman was particularly cheerful about that historic policy. For the first time, a ruling approved by FERC said they can determine the "diverse range of potential benefits from proposals to integrate state-determined carbon pricing into the regional markets."

Here's what that means. For carbon emissions, the Neil Chatterjee led Commission said that states that place a value on carbon emissions, as they have done in California and the ten states that comprise the Regional Greenhouse Gas Initiative, fall under FERC oversight. No longer, apparently, is carbon emission the province of states here and there. It now has a federal father who goes by the name of FERC.

To gain an appreciation of how bold a move this is, you may recall the Trump Administration hounded California because of its auto emission standards which were first adopted in 2004[10] both to reduce tailpipe emissions and improve gas mileage well above what the federal standard was. Instead of treating California and RGGI as outliers needing to be hemmed, FERC's decision to embrace carbon emission reductions adopted by those states was, well, an incredible precedent. Chatterjee asserted that carbon oversight wasn't an overreach but, rather, an adoption of a market approach to pricing what a ton of carbon emission would fetch. Said another way, Chatterjee saw the number of states adopting various versions of carbon emission-related efforts and decided that a patchwork of pricing schemes would be better handled on a national effort similar to how FERC adjudicates transmission rates.

A template has now been set for the Biden Administration to start collecting revenues for the eventuality of a carbon emissions market that are needed to pay the freight on the new president's $2 trillion climate effort.

The overview led to Chatterjee's response to the now persistent question posed by the 21st Century Committee, "Can we do it again?" Well, perhaps, Chatterjee replied, but "only if the co-op model which seems to resist public policy at every turn changes." Citing from a menu of FERC orders, is this one provocatively called 841.[11] That policy deals with energy storage which gives batteries equal footing with fossil fuel generation. Chatterjee said NRECA sued FERC to ensure its members were largely exempted. That didn't happen as disappointed NRECA CEO Jim Mathison said: "The commission has dealt a blow to consumers and dramatically expanded its authority by giving itself the discretion to decide which distributed and behind the meter energy storage resources can participate in wholesale electricity markets."[12]

The co-ops did a bit better with yet another numerical FERC Order, this one #2222.[13] This numerical alliteration treats distributed energy resources like demand side management in the same fashion as mammoth generators. You might call this PURPA 2.0—the Jimmy Carter energy effort requiring utilities to purchase the power output from Elon Musk's electric car discharging its battery storage load back into the grid. The co-ops received an opt-out from FERC which agreed that meeting Order 2222 was well beyond what they could handle. Larger co-ops and G&Ts, however, could opt-in should they choose to do so.

Chatterjee added that the pace of changes in carbon emission markets and the involvement of non-traditional sources of generation, micro grids, and the like will only accelerate. For co-ops to be obstinate about those rules means their views won't receive the consideration other entrants might have when their points of view are recognized.

Remaining theoretical, Chatterjee responded to the inquiry of what he would do if, say, he was the CEO of a major coal-based G&T. "At the end of the day," the Chairman noted, "rates have to be affordable and the delivery reliable." Channeling his inner G&T, Chatterjee added a caveat already acknowledged in the co-op community that G&Ts and distribution co-ops must acknowledge the changing energy choices of their customer base and act accordingly.[14] The Chairman noted the fleeting view that coal remains cheap and the fear of stranding large generation assets posed a daunting challenge for G&Ts. However, at the end of yet another day, G&Ts need to look at the math to measure the economics of maintaining its coal fleet. While he didn't mention it, GRE's retirement of its 1,200 MW Coal Creek station saw the math to do so and the accountants that are the GRE board decided management was right to phase that plant out.

Perhaps the FERC orders to count distributed energy as a resource, as is true with energy storage, is the course G&Ts need to follow if indeed they can muster the energy to acknowledge they an do it again. If not, the eventual adoption of a carbon emissions market, and assuredly there will be one, may well cause co-ops to be adrift of the national mood.

Ah, the national mood. The next chapter details then President Obama's clean power plan initiative solely designed to reduce carbon emissions. While much of that was accomplished by switching from lumps lining some Christmas stockings to natural gas, the demand to arrest carbon emissions will only accelerate. Chatterjee sees his legacy as FERC oversight of an eventual carbon market. While some states will resist any type of state action on carbon, and you know who you are, their utilities will not have the same luxury given FERC under the Federal Power Act that clearly has jurisdiction over much of their activities including transmission scheduling and rates. Co-ops, likewise, will be part of that oversight, particularly if they seek FERC jurisdiction as did Tri-State.

The irony, of course, is that some co-ops seeking their G&T leave may do so because of carbon concerns. Seeking FERC jurisdiction to dissuade the recalcitrant will force G&Ts to become FERC compliant, a view that not all that long ago was anathema. Keep in mind and, of course, that is nearly impossible to-do, critics of the electric cooperatives may well be providing the answer to the question many co-ops frequently wonder of can we do it again.?"

Keep Chatterjee in mind as one of those who provided a blueprint to do so.

Chapter 21

Abiding Biden

L et's get biblical, again, for the moment. Matthew 25:7 is the parable of the ten virgins minding their lamps which was necessary for the bridegrooms to come and fetch them. The ten hoped instead for an LED, which was a bit delayed. The point of that Gospel is lamps, or that lights are a symbol of guidance.[1] Here's the guidance you're about to see.

In August of 2015, President Obama signed an Executive Order entitled, Clean Power Plan.[2] If you don't recall what all of that covered in the waning days of the Obama Administration, we're going to refresh that carbon dating memory.

The CPP assigned each state an individual goal for reducing their carbon emissions and they included:

- North Dakota, Wyoming, Montana, Minnesota, Wisconsin, Iowa, Illinois, and Kansas were required to reduce carbon emissions equal to or greater than 41 percent.
- South Dakota, Nebraska, Washington, Utah, Arizona, New Mexico, Texas, Georgia, Arkansas, Tennessee, Alabama, North and South Carolina, West Virginia, Ohio, Pennsylvania, Oklahoma, and Indiana clocked in at 31–40 percent reduction.
- Don't see your state? You are still looking at knocking off carbon exhalation up to 30 percent.[3]

The ensuing controversy among coal-dependent states was led by West Virginia which filed suit prompting the Supreme Court to stay the entire plan. The Court argued that the proposal exceeded the EPA's mandate under the Clean Air Act and violated states' rights to regulate electric power.[4] The

Supreme Court tied on that one leaving the stay in place but not answering the question whether or not EPA had the right to regulate carbon emissions under the Clean Air Act. That question was never answered after President Trump directed then EPA Director Scott Pruitt to scuttle the entire works.

Biden said on his first day in office that he'll rejoin the Paris Accord intended to keep the world from heating another 2° Celsius by 2100. Here's what the US would have to do:[5]

- Provide $3 billion to the Green Climate Fund.
- Reduce US carbon emissions 26 to 28 percent below 2005 levels by 2025.

To that, President Biden also created the Climate 21 Project[6] which includes the US Department of Agriculture that attentive readers will recall houses RUS. The list of federal participants also includes The Justice Department, Department of Interior, EPA, Department of Transportation, Office of Management and Budget, and the US Treasury. Here's what Climate 21, not to be confused with Century 21, wants to do:

- Eliminate carbon emission from the electric sector by 2035
- Achieve overall net zero carbon emission by 2050
- Resumption of the CAFE program for corporate average fuel economy standards, meaning for every Ford F150 there will be an offsetting smart car
- By 2030 all buses will be electric powered
- Additional research into carbon capture and recovery, technology now being pursued by two North Dakota G&Ts, Basin Electric and Minnkota Electric
- Create an Environmental and Climate Justice Division within the Justice Department

West Virginia and others might prevail in any effort preventing EPA to Posse Comitatus carbon emissions given the conservative composition of the Supreme Court. Then again, it might not matter when you consider that thirty states have various renewable energy portfolios, carbon emission mandates, and decreasing energy usage laws. All of those contribute to the Climate 21 goal of zero carbon emissions for industry by 2035.

Here we must throw out an analogy. In the 1980s, A&W tried to compete with McDonald's quarter pounder by selling a one-third pounder at a lower cost. That burger failed because most customers thought the quarter pounder was bigger.[7] If you fall into that camp, no need to keep reading. If not, here's more cautionary observations.

FERC has already issued a proposed policy statement to clarify that it has jurisdiction over organized wholesale electric market rules that incorporate a state-determined carbon price in those markets. While not a mandate, that market approach may prompt Appalachian Power, conveniently located in Almost Heaven, West Virginia,[8] little choice but to capitulate to the carbon market FERC may well be minding.

Most electric cooperatives, even with the Trump Administration vowing to make coal great again, have worked hard to reduce their stockpile of carbon emissions. They did so either through relying more on natural gas, shifting to wind, banking on carbon capture and sequestration technology, investing in solar, or flat out saying, as did Tri-State, that it will cut emissions by 80 percent within ten years.[9] According to a 2017 NRECA fact sheet, co-ops nationally have reduced carbon emissions by 9 percent.[10] With various plant closures, like GRE's Coal Creek, and Tri-State's proposed carbon Nicoderm patch, it appears co-ops may be in accord with the Paris Accord reductions of 26–28 percent below 2005 levels by 2025 but not quite carbon free by 2035.

RUS will not be responsive to any coal-bent generation. You need only look to 2008 when Speaker Pelosi and then Energy and Commerce Chair Henry Waxman raised concerns about the financial risks associated with carbon emissions, prompting RUS to suspend loans for coal-based activities.[11] More recently, in 2020 the Federal Reserve for the first time called out "climate change among risks enumerated in its biannual financial stability report and warned about the potential for abrupt changes in asset values in response to a warming planet."[12]

As daunting as excising CO_2 is, even more difficult for co-ops is to change their culture. Admittedly, the co-op culture has been widely successful, prompting so many to invoke the banality about breakage. However, know this. A Biden Administration is intent on social change, on social justice, on equality, on black lives matter, and everything those ethics if not edicts suggest and the civil rights audit last seen in the waning days of 2001 may well be implemented. If so, it's likely that co-ops not much liking RUS telling them their boards don't reflect the membership have the option of being 100 percent borrowers of CFC as is already true with 250 co-ops. Yet the federal reach is long and includes perhaps requiring REDLG recipients to fall in line with RUS-prescribed social dictates. CFC can borrow from the Federal Financing Bank under what's called the Guaranteed Underwriting Program to make loans to their member co-ops. As part of that program, CFC also pays fees based on the amount borrowed to fund REDLG. An attentive USDA Secretary, let alone RUS Administrator, could insist that the co-ops' economic development efforts through REDLG ensure the boards applying for those loans or grants reflect the communities they serve if not being attentive to loan requests from minority-owned businesses.

It is the same federal ploy used to ensure that states follow highway speed limits. Montana highways at one time resembled the Autobahn. The Big Sky state, when threatened with the loss of highway funds, decided seventy-five miles per hour was fast enough. Said another way, most sources of financing that co-ops tap may have a federal taint, meaning the government is positioned to reach into the board rooms. Think not?

Think about this: California, as detailed in Chapter 6 is proposing corporate boards include slots for women. You can scoff that this is affirmative action but it is an action of affirmation that corporate boards must have a balance. The same, as has been hectored in various chapters, is also true for co-ops. The Federal government—be it through loans, regulations, or regulatory agencies like FERC—can dictate that recipients of federal assistance, and that includes every co-op in one way or another, have to show a social balance on their boards and perhaps their work force. If not the feds, then the states which already regulate co-ops on any number of levels may be poised to do the same thing.

That is already being done on the environmental front, either prompted by state policy or increasingly by G&T boards that see clearly that the future will not be much inhabited by carbon emissions. You, of course, know that. Attendance at NRECA statewide meetings and, increasingly, zoom calls feature little else but loosening the carbon bonds. Those co-op imbued trade associations are unfortunately a bit too reticent about the necessity to talk about the importance of black lives matter, that a board's responsibility means inclusion, that the absence of people of color reduce the realm of possibilities co-ops cannot afford among so many reasons why the S in environmental social governance is critical. The S, or social, includes, "Diversity and inclusion in hiring and in awarding advancement opportunities and raises."[13]

Here's what was said in Chapter 9: "Environment-social-governance responsibility investment, the most notable called the Climate Action 100,[14] now surpasses some $32 trillion dollars. Ask yourself, would that fund find your local electric cooperative to be sufficiently ESG or, said another way, does your co-op meet the parameters the 21st Century Cooperative Committee envisioned?"

In the final chapter, we will lay out the tenets of how a co-op can get there.

Chapter 22

2200 BC

Today, they're called customer service representatives, or Member Service Directors, but as late as the 1980s, they were called Power Use Advisors, giving advice on all things electric. Early annual meetings saw arrays of ovens, stoves, refrigerators, and later on irrigation pumps. Co-op members would ask the Power Use Advisor a great many questions on what to buy, how to hook it up, and then would argue whether Allis Chamber was a better tractor than John Deere. Since then, the conversation centers on electric vehicles, solar panels, cycling air conditioning, and off-peak programs provided, of course, that the co-op remains the member's trust energy advisor. For the most part, co-ops have been the advisors and for good reasons.

An earlier chapter entitled The New Green Deal detailed how co-ops have converted water heaters into one very large Delco battery, interrupted irrigation to avoid paying peak electric rates and conserving water, and recapturing the members' interest in renewable energy and invigorating the members' appreciation of the co-op which provides broadband.

The 21st Century Electric Cooperative envisioned by Mike Williams's Committee needs repeating and is summarized by this checklist:

1. Co-ops need to reach out to their individual members, each and every one
2. If you don't do it, others will
3. Co-ops can help new construction to finance energy conservation improvements
4. How co-ops can customize the members' electric usage
5. How co-ops can transition from an AT&T behemoth to an innovative iPhone utility

6. Improving a co-op's load factor by enticing electric vehicle saturation
7. Solar coupled with storage alters the economics of electricity
8. Think like a young consumer
9. Reimagine the customer's electric use
10. What the 21st Century Electric Cooperative can mean to your members

Let's go back in time, however, to water mains that first appeared in 2200 BC. We've cited the Institute for Local Self Reliance on voting matters but their proposal using water mains as a substitute for ground source heat pumps offers one of the great load building and membership outreach efforts for co-ops. Here's how ILSR describes itself:

"The Institute for Local Self-Reliance (ILSR) is a national nonprofit research and educational organization founded in 1974. ILSR has a vision of thriving, diverse, equitable communities. To reach this vision, we build local power to fight corporate control. We believe that democracy can only thrive when economic and political power is widely dispersed. Whether it's fighting back against the outsize power of monopolies like Amazon or advocating to keep local renewable energy in the community that produced it, ILSR advocates for solutions that harness the power of citizens and communities." More at www.ilsr.org.[1]

Here's their idea:[2]

"Air source heat pumps can replace existing fossil-powered systems, but struggle to compete cost-effectively in cold climates. Water main geothermal combines the efficiency and technical capability of ground-source geothermal in cold climates with costs competitive to fossil gas furnaces. Using a heat exchanger attached to the water main (or a short spur), this mechanism replaces expensive well drilling or expansive loop fields to deliver thermal energy to a building's geothermal heat pump.

Water main geothermal could provide a viable, cost-effective alternative to traditional home heating and cooling systems. Homeowners benefit from lower heating and cooling costs, water utilities benefit from a new source of income, and cities benefit from reaching their climate commitments."

Not mentioned, but equally important, is the co-op's role as power advisor to do or facilitate the installation and provide the financing as electric cooperatives have done for the far more expensive ground source heat pumps.

The authors John Farrell and Lilly Ambort report that heating and cooling of the nation's homes account for 440 million tons of CO_2 annually.[3] Think again of the carbon-backed IRA concept and how using water mains as a heat pump could help fund your members' flagging IRA, build load, and affirm to the members just how vital the co-op is to them.

Ground source heat pumps require a well field where coils are dropped into the aquifer to take advantage of the constant 50 or so degree of underground water. On average, heat pumps knock off a bit more than 40 percent of the electric bill, principally because heat pumps produce more energy than they use.[4] The payback, however, can stretch upward to ten years. The solution to the cost of ground source heat pumps which can cost between \$12,000 and \$20,000[5] is to tap into the water main.

To see the graphics for how one school did so, tap into the www.ilsr.org web site[6] but, as they describe it, the water from the main flows into the heat exchanger which extracts heat in the winter or cooling in the summer for the glycol loop serving the building. The heated or cooled water/glycol solution then travels to the geothermal heat pump units serving classrooms. After the heat exchanger extracts or returns heat, the water from the main goes to the sanitary sewer and a diffusion well that returns the water to the local aquifer.[7] Yeah, well, your co-op guys will know exactly how to construct that loop.

The authors correctly note that water utilities could make cake by offering up their water mains for heat pumps to, among other things, finance aging infrastructure. Or the co-op could do so in concert with the water utility which in most cases is owned by the local municipality. Here's the estimated cost for a home spread over 2,000 square feet according to the authors:[8]

"The cost of a water main geothermal system for a homeowner connecting to the municipal water main, installing a standard three-ton system with a double-wall heat exchanger, and a geothermal heat pump would be $6,000 to $12,000 depending on the efficiency of the system. Installing traditional geothermal in a typical 2,000 square foot home costs around $20,000. Currently, there is a 26 percent tax credit from the IRS on all geothermal system equipment. In 2021, it will decrease to 22 percent and may expire if not renewed by the end of the year. The added financial incentives and tax benefits cut the cost of geothermal systems even further. In connecting geothermal heat pumps to the water main, tax credits cut the cost of installation from over $14,000 to less than $9,000. If the water utility provides the infrastructure necessary for a new spur from the water main and the heat exchanger, the cost of the system decreases to less than $6,000. As noted, the cost of ground source heat pumps starts at something a bit more.

The electricity needed to energize the water main heat pump, according to the authors, is an estimated 6,520 kWh. You can do the math based on the retail cost of your co-op and potentially reducing that if the heat pump is subject to load control. Here's the summary:

Water main geothermal systems could cut the cost of installing a geothermal system in half. At the lower price, it reduces costs compared to air source heat pumps and oil furnaces while providing cost competitive savings compared to gas furnaces. Water main geothermal systems could cut electricity usage between 25 percent to 50 percent and reduce emissions by up to 85 percent compared to traditional HVAC systems. Water main geothermal is one of the most cost effective and environmentally friendly ways to heat and cool residential homes.

Finally, "An often-overlooked benefit of electrification, such as transitioning from fossil gas furnaces to heat pumps, is the opportunity to produce the energy for heating and cooling locally or on site. Approximately 40 percent of American homes are suitable for solar and every household could own a slice of a community solar project nearby. In both cases, the solar electricity could power the heat pump for heating and cooling the building. A typical 5 kilowatt residential solar array in the Midwest would produce enough electricity each year to entirely offset the additional electricity demand for heating from a heat pump.

"The heat pump opportunity also suggests a change to solar policy. Electricity customers with solar are often required to size their solar array to the home's electricity use. Net metering allows customers to subtract from their electric bill all the electricity they produce, paying just the net amount. But size limits associated with net metering, in theory to prevent customers from overproducing, do not account for the growing use of electricity to power everything. A heat pump increases electricity use even as it reduces overall energy consumption for heating. An electric vehicle does the same. Since customer-sited solar has significant social and environmental benefits, electricity consumers argue for allowing them to be maximized in size to serve existing and future electricity uses."

Since nothing is ever easy, the authors said these questions need to be answered:

1. What state or local rules may impede implementation including health department regulations or plumbing codes?
2. What is the temperature of the water, size of the water main, and rate of water flow needed for proper heat exchange?
3. What neighborhoods already have existing water infrastructure and flow rates that would handle heat exchange?
4. What parts of the water distribution system are already scheduled for upgrades?
5. What are the estimated costs of upgrading the water mains needed to implement the geothermal connection?
6. How much would it cost to install a double-walled heat exchanger and perhaps a geothermal heat pump for 100 homes or 1,000 homes? Could the city afford to pay the upfront costs and recoup the cost on the water bill?

7. What kind of technical or financial assistance can be offered to residents for installing a geothermal heat pump and a double-walled heat exchanger?
8. What is the best starting point for this system to be implemented in the city? Would it focus on commercial buildings or residential?
9. How long is the cost recovery for water infrastructure upgrades for the water utility?
10. How much revenue would be generated for the water utility?
11. What are the health, safety, and environmental benefits for the city and its residents such as carbon emissions reductions, indoor air quality, and reduced risk of gas leaks which are all questions the co-op could and should answer.
12. What are the overall economic and financial benefits for both the city and the residents?

Then again, the effort to install broadband, finance ground source heat pumps, entice members to allow the co-ops to control loads, market DirecTV, and install Wild Blue dishes among the many programs and services co-ops have offered throughout the years took effort. Tapping into water mains to save members considerable money and providing the opportunity to cash in carbon savings for deflated retirement accounts, and to do so through community solar gardens if not rooftop solar, is what a twenty-first century co-op is.

Chapter 23

Aspiration Electrification

Lowndes County is located in the Black Belt of Alabama. The New Yorker called Lowndes County as "one of the poorest counties in one of America's poorest states."[1] Dixie Electric, located in Union Springs, serves a part of that county among the eight counties the co-op lines extend into.

According to The New Yorker article, 40 percent of the households have an inadequate septic system or none with many of those homes discharging raw sewage, a practice called straight piping. Parasites and hookworms are a result of straight piping. In 2017, Baylor researchers discovered hookworms in more than a third of Lowndes County residents.[2]

Earlier, the cost was recounted to provide a rural customer with electricity and broadband. Wastewater is far more expensive. According to the Water/ Wastewater Superintendent for the city of Washougal, Washington, extending wastewater services to serve say, 5,000 residents of Lowndes County, Alabama over 100 miles of trunk line would cost an estimated $92 million or an estimated $18,480 per customer.[3] Dixie Electric or any other co-op simply cannot afford to cover the cost of that infrastructure. Sadly, the same is true with individual septic systems which are dependent on soil type. Sandy soil means a system costing around $2,500. The clay-like soil pervasive in Lowndes County increases that cost per septic system nearly tenfold.

The USDA did provide a $23 million grant to the city of Union Town. That grant will extend upgraded sewer service to 2,810 residents[4] with few, it appears, living in Lowndes County.

You may recall that the Trump Administration promised to spend a trillion dollars on infrastructure, which never happened. Doing so may well have stopped the leakage of sewage into desperately poor county residents' yards.

Water, however, didn't seem to be a problem and for that Dixie Electric is one reason why.

Gary Harrison is the CEO of Dixie Electric. Here's what he told the author: "I will tell you that Dixie was one of the first co-ops in the United States (mid 1970s) to develop a management agreement and start operating a rural water system. We actually helped found the Alabama Rural Water Association and our water superintendent is the current chairman. He also serves on the national rural water association board for Alabama. We did get proposals for our water system, South Bullock, several years ago to develop a sewer system. Due to the lack of density, the cost could not be justified at the time.[5]

Harrison said Dixie prefers to work in concert with other entities that have more expertise in ventures important to co-op members. Harrison observed that Dixie has aligned with local telephone cooperatives along with rural water systems because not only do they know that business end better than Dixie, but they are also RUS borrowers. Those with attentive memories may recall that was a theme of Chapter 19 entitled, Musing Mergers, not to mention the cooperative commandment of working with other cooperatives.

Dixie Electric—and there are two, the other one located in Mississippi—is also somewhat of an anomaly in that its board includes several directors of color. Harrison affirmed that his board's diversity is advantageous as it broadens the co-op to the consider sundry needs of its members. Harrison also took pride that the co-op's workforce also resembled the membership.[6] That is the genesis of an electrification aspiration cooperative. Addressing a need within a co-op's ability to do so is an affirmative answer to yes, we can do so, and is amplified by a board with diverse backgrounds reflecting the views of its members. But there's more than that and here comes the heavy lifting.

Aspiration-oriented cooperatives need to define leadership. Each year NRECA holds a contest asking applicants to list how their co-op is meeting the cooperative difference and to include evidence of practicing the cooperative principals. The contest named for J. C. Brown, the long-ago editor of the RE Newsletter, further inquires about a co-op's strategic plan and how the CEO communicates that forward thinking document. Two other categories ask how the CEO supports the co-op's communicators and the success of the co-op's chitchat efforts.

In 2020, thirteen co-ops applied. Hardly a representative sampling but perhaps an indicator that co-op CEOs see themselves as caretakers more than leaders. Entrants, representing .015 of the 850 some co-ops, stressed their leadership credentials. That includes embracing change, innovation, and fidelity to long-term planning.

Do co-op CEOs contemplate the long run into this century? That doesn't necessarily mean thinking about the new generational SCADA system. While important, it doesn't necessarily think what the membership needs and how to deliver it.

During the 2020 Oregon Statewide annual meeting delivered over zoom, the futurist Glenn Hiemstra said this decade will be the most intensive ten years that co-ops have faced. Hiemstra trotted out the stuff we know: EVs, solar, improved battery life, and the growth of industrial sized wind turbines. Those sources can easily be met by competitors and they already are. What can't be met is serving the likes of Lowndes County. Doing so is the call of co-ops, hopefully in a collaborative way, because few have the appetite to do so.

In a bit we'll get to twenty-five aspirations your co-op might contemplate. No. 24 cites a fifteen-year-old girl by the name of Gitanjali Rao. She invented an app on her iPhone, and now on yours, to test for lead in drinking water. Surely there are people as innovative as Ms. Rao who could come up with ways to address wastewater system problems.

Here's one final preachy observation. The country faces multiple crises simultaneously and COVID-19 is simply the most recent and immediate. There are the ravages of climate change, an utterly broken political system, a vacuum in global leadership, gross disparities in affluence and influence, and on and on. Co-ops were created to make a difference. There is an urgency to do so in this century.

Here's what else aspirational may mean to your cooperative:

1. Every electric cooperative met area coverage decades ago. Now co-ops are assessing whether or not there is sufficient interest for broadband. Earlier, CFC estimated that perhaps 20 percent of co-ops can do so given the cost and the competition that likely has hawked the good loads. Instead, the USDA State Director

has extensive information on unmet needs like wastewater, water, septic systems, and other utility infrastructure that may well be met by the co-ops.

2. Here's a tough one: Does the co-op board resemble the membership? While most rural, and that's what they are, electric cooperatives' memberships are predominantly older and white, the co-op could take affirmative steps to develop a bench of younger members, if not members of color, who can assume a director position following retirement.

3. On that theme, the NRECA and CFC treatise on governance is outstanding. They, however, should go further. Governance is about representation and if the co-op isn't adequately representing its membership, then a tract on co-op governance should clearly spell that out and offer solutions. We are quite aware of the bromide that an electric co-op trade association can only dance with the ones that brung them. Better said in this day and in this age, is that Statewides and NRECA should lead that dance.

4. NRECA offers board evaluations which, if truth be told, are likely watered down. That doesn't make the co-op board any different from most corporate boards. However, it does offer an opportunity for the twenty-first century co-op board to do a realistic examination of those who contribute and those that don't. Contribution is, of course, a subjective term but a willingness to address the hard truths of climate change or the necessity to embrace the needs of a diverse membership isn't.

5. In some cases, the name of a co-op also speaks of the co-op's mission statement. Naming a co-op after a county speaks of geography and not purpose. Embracing a name that harkens to confederacy or named for an outdated historical term deprecates whatever forward program is embraced by the co-op. Contemplate changing the name to celebrate a defining trait of the co-op's service area.

6. Nationally, 89 percent of the population like renewables. Meeting that favorability factor will be near impossible if the co-op's all

requirement contract is titled toward coal. Not only should the co-op advocate for renewable energy but it should do so well beyond the 5 percent limitation allowed by many G&Ts.

7. Nearly every co-op utters the phrase, "We are owned by the members we serve." How about currying that membership for sources of renewable energy they have developed? Recall the 21st Century Committee observation that the co-op only needs 15 percent of the membership to remain relevant? Buying local brings the locals around.

8. So does a program that rewards member's efforts to reduce their carbon exposure. The Carbon IRA provides monetary inducement to help co-ops meet state carbon reductions if not that which may well be mandated by the federal government.

9. The 21st Century Committee observed that the average electric cooperative is engaged in some thirty-one social outreach efforts. What are they and what, perhaps, has a more pressing purpose?

10. Statewides and NRECA are very attentive to what their members want. To date, that mostly has been to tell legislators and regulators to leave them be. That simply won't work anymore. Co-ops must tell their trade associations to embrace renewables and to support electrification that is absent a sizable carbon content. Not doing so means being stuck with a plan that may be averse to the co-op.

11. Perhaps tapping the water main as a heat pump doesn't work for your co-op. What does? Co-ops have had huge success marketing water heaters as storage for wind energy.

12. G&Ts include very smart people who can and have negotiated favorable wind and solar contracts. G&Ts have resources that are well beyond the reach of most of their members. They already know virtually everything about co-ops. If you want to go PURPA with your members, then the G&T is best positioned to help you do so. Ditching the G&T for another suitor may provide Maslow-like satisfaction but, in the long run, the new boss is the same as the old boss. Said less lyrically, the G&T eventually bends

to meet the needs of the membership which was demonstrated by Tri-State and Great River Energy.

13. Still, there will be co-ops thinking they can do better for their membership alone. Perhaps they can. However, they need to know the number of dollars for that particular freedom. Any number of consulting firms are ready to supply that exit fee. The G&T community should coalesce around a defensible number and one that holds harmless the other committee G&T members.

14. To that, Chapter 11 proposed a course design for G&T directors. That shouldn't be ignored.

15. Cooperative evangelism up to this point is the province of evangelists like Bill Collet and CFC who've convinced IOUs and some municipalities to sell out to acquisitive co-ops. Think of the inducement your co-op could offer IOU members clamoring for a cleaner source of electricity. There's no better way to enliven interest in becoming a co-op member than offering services others desire.

16. On that note, do NRECA and CFC want to take another run at forming 1st Rochdale Electric Cooperative? Its been more than twenty years since that urban experiment, a time when the G&T developed a robust power trading floor called ACEs. The development of Regional Transmission Organizations likewise provide a source of generation that didn't much exist back in 1998. Doing so portends many potential opportunities including the support of a sizable Congressional delegation.

17. Look at least at what mergers in your Statewide might mean. Ask your Statewide to develop a scenario of super co-ops. Then follow up that exercise with the critical question of what can we do collectively, i.e., through mergers, that we can't do individually?

18. Up until recently, co-ops were a bunch of utilities. We need to continue that backslapping tradition not only among our guys but among those not much like us. Meet with homeless shelters to understand how a co-op can facilitate housing options. There's no deficit of groups representing that societal concern. Howdy

them, and see what a co-op can do for them. If your co-op has a large minority population, you best invite them to hear how the co-op can incorporate their views if not their needs.

19. The opioid crisis is just that. Co-op line workers go into areas otherwise seldom visited. Are they equipped to administer naloxone should the need arise?

20. Are you paying attention to co-op critics like We Own It or the Local Institute for Self-Reliance that have taken it upon themselves to point out aspects of the co-op operation or organization needing attention? We don't much like critics but their overview, no matter how adverse, may make a co-op a much more responsive utility for their members. Need we remind the reader that the co-op is all about the member?

21. The answer to can we do it and can we do it again is best addressed by the phenomenal success of the Kauai Island Utility Cooperative. First formed in 2002, the co-op has the highest percentage of renewable energy coursing through their lines. KIUC also partners with health services that among other things provides rental and mortgage assistance. They have an incredible story to tell. Invite them to Bismarck or Pierre or Nashville or any of your population centers to see what the Island Co-op has done that perhaps you can do as well.

22. Chapter 7 covers what we could have done on climate change. Perhaps you recall how the Institute for Self-Reliance told how the $6 billion lending authority could be used for the renewable generation. Then think how well that would be embraced by a RUS under the Biden Administration. To be sure, co-ops need those billions for maintenance, extensions, and transmission for renewables. We also could use the additional dough to assist members who want to be carbon neutral. Here's the tag line for that. "Brought to you by your local electric cooperative."

23. Chapter 3 was the best chapter to write because it reflects what co-ops have done to meet, among so many things, Sermon on the Mount dictates. That chapter heading, We're the Helpers,

resonates with so many because it speaks to being part of something, rural electrification, that is so much bigger than the rest of us. That's what aspiration is all about—aspiring to do great things. This book, this chapter, is all about desiring to do even better.

24. A fifteen-year-old girl by the name of Gitanjali Rao was named Time Magazine's Kid of the Year. The Colorado teenager invented a mobile device to test for lead in drinking water.[7] While a young women of that intellect may not live in each co-op service area, there exists, nonetheless, many many exceptionally bright individuals who have ideas to assist a co-op. To ferret them out and to reward their efforts, co-ops might contemplate advertising for ideas to further broadband, or renewable energy, or carbon capture, or cost-effective water and wastewater systems among the opportunities the co-op could pursue. The co-op is comprised of the members. The co-op should ask their members what cool projects they can deliver for the entire membership's benefit.

25. We can't do it alone. The heartbreak of inadequate sewer systems recounted in that New Yorker article simply cannot be handled singularly by a co-op. The same may be true with other offerings like broadband or water or any number of services desperately needed by rural residents. Working in concert with others, however, may bridge those economic barriers. That is the sixth commandment, not that religious one but the cooperative principle of working with cooperatives or apostates if necessary.

The 21st Century Committee produced one of NRECA's most important documents of all time. That Committee not only asked the critical question of whether the co-ops want to remain relevant but how should they get there. We hope this book helps answers those questions.

The doing is up to you.

Acknowledgments

There are 31,202 bible passages. My favorite, the last Chapter of the last verse of John features books: "And there are also many other things which Jesus did, the which, if they should be written every-one, I suppose that even the world itself could not contain the books that should be written."

Here's a listing of those who wrote meaningful chapters for me: Al Ballard, Rex Carpenter, Paul Neil, Margaret Bacon, Ron Holstein, the Nebraska Rural Electric Association, Bob Patridge, Bob Bergland, Carolyn Herr Watts, Jean McKinney, Jere Overs, Chuck Fadeley, Dave Harper, Chuck Gill, Chub Ulmer, Sheldon Petersen, Rich LaRochelle, Glen English, Tom Fennel, Howard and Rick Crinklaw, Jack Heaston, Bob Speckman, Jim Stubblefield, Dave Sabala, Art Thomsen, Sara Baker-Sifford, Laura Waterman, John Mayse, Jim Ramseyer, Ed Schlender, Russ Dorran, Ted Perry, Don Walker, Norm Oakley, John Sims, Peggi Timm and the Oregon Rural Electric Cooperative Association.

My Rural Electric Statewide colleagues: Tom Jones, Dennis Hill, Dave Wheelihan, Frank Stork, Barry Hart, Ray Clifton, Jay Downen, Ron Sheets, Ray Kuhl, Paul Wood, Hobson Waits, Tom Purkey, Bill Willingham, Fred Clark, Brian Kading, Marilyn Leland, Shawn Taylor, Keven Groenwold, Steve Brame, Bill Corum, Jessica Nelson, Ken Kaylor, Share Brandt, Duane Noland, Michael Callahan, Craig Borr, Kent Singer, Ted Case, Jay Holmquist Chris Meyers, Nell Hotchkiss, Michael Couick, Ed Anderson, Wes Ehrecke, Dave Callis, Mike Peterson, Wally Rustad, Kent Lopez and in particular, Mike Williams.

Minnesota occupies a huge place in my heart including Peter Wojciechowski, Norm Krause, Fran Bator, Carl Potter,, Harvey Hesse, Mark Vogt, Rik Banke,

Mike Bash, Roger Geckler, Mark Laub, Greg Miller, Bruce Bjerke, Jim Krueger, Steve Shurts, Tim SullivanTom Malone, Tim Thompson, Tim O'Leary, Mike Adams, Jeff Nelson, Tim Mergen, Brian Krambeer, Ryan Hentges, Garry Bye, Linda Laitala, Lidia Jacobson, Ron Schwartau, Wes Waller, Dan Hoskins, Ron Horman, DeeAnne Newville, Syd Briggs, Robin Doege, Jerry Mevissen, Steve Haaven, Charles Riesen, Steve Arnesen, Mac McLennan, Stacey Dahl, Ron Kennedy, Dave Saggau, Tom Graham, Dave Sogard, TomWoinarowicz, Jeff Redalen, Jim Cox, Gary Connett,, Jill Beighley, Mike Rajala, Dave George, Roger Johanneck, Stacy Dahl, Will Kaul, Elaine Garry, Jeff Folland, Amy Fredregill, Gene Sullivan, Hap Levander, Wade Hensel, Marty Hillert, Kenric Scheevel, Audrey Hjelle, Dave Minge, and really, the Minnesota Rural Electric membership that never failed to inspire me or make me laugh.

Special thanks to my brilliant employees at MREA: Aleia Yue, Alison Deelstra, Lee Sundberg, Melissa Stackovich, Mary Alice Holm,Beth Knudson, Sandy Soweija, Joel Johnson, Grania McKernan, Tom Harrel, Sally Ryman, along with people I really liked: Jim Berstein, Lois Mack, Al Franken, Tim Walz, Amy Klobuchar, Bob Buckler, Bob Szabo, Gil Gutknecht, Steve Tomac, Mike Eggl, Kirk Johnson, Terry Bruns, Luis Reyes, Jeff Almen, Steve Collier, Andy Brown, Jeff Harrison, Bob Phillips, Bob Marshall, Jason Makansi, Laura Schepis, Steve Jueck, Billy Hoffman, Laura Waterman, Bill Collet, Vern Dosch, Bill Mullan, Debra Sliz, Nivin Elgohary, Phil Irwin, Brad Janorschke, Susan Olander Tom Graves, Jim Horan, Rich Larochelle, Jason Makansi, Martin Lowery, Jerry Bingold, Adam Schwarts, and if I missed you, I will apologize for the rest of my life for that egregious omission.

To that, are those who made this book possible: editor Joan Sands and book designer Vinnie Kinsella.

And, my family, noted earlier, but their support and talent deserve another mention: Debbie, Molly, Casey and Cody, their spouses Kelly and Valon and my beguiling grandchildren: Dash, Patrick, Phineas, Eliott and Darla. If I may, again, my Mom and Dad, Herman and Ruth Glaess who I owe so very much and to my sisters, Anita, twin Marian and Lori.

Endnotes

Introduction: Faith is like electricity. You can't see it, but you can see the light.

1. Jill Lepore, "Democracy in Peril, Then and Now," *New Yorker*, February 3, 2020.
2. Edmund Morris, *Edison* (New York: Random House, 2019), 370.
3. Harold Severson, *The Night They Turned on the Lights* (Midwest Historical Features, 1962).
4. Richard Rudolph and Scott Ridley, *Power Struggle: The Hundred-Year War over Electricity* (New York: Harper & Row, 1986), 80–81.
5. Richard A. Pence, ed., *The Next Greatest Thing* (Washington, DC: National Rural Electric Cooperative Association, 1984), dust jacket overview.
6. Ibid.
7. Robert Caro, *The Years of Lyndon Johnson: The Path To Power* (New York: Random House), 504.
8. Rudolph and Ridley, *Power Struggle,* 79.
9. Ibid.
10. "Rural Electrification Act (REA) (1935)," The Living New Deal, accessed September 16, 2021, https://livingnewdeal.org/glossary/rural-electrification-administration-rea-1935/.
11. Ibid.
12. Richard Pence and Patrick Dahl, *The Next Greatest Thing* (Washington, DC: National Rural Electric Cooperative Association, 1984), book cover citation.
13. "Franklin D. Roosevelt > Quotes > Quotable Quote," Goodreads, accessed September 16, 2021, https://www.goodreads.com/quotes/35186-the-test-of-our-progress-is-not-whether-we-add.
14. Arthur M. Schlesinger Jr., *The Age of Roosevelt: The Politics of Upheaval* (Boston: Houghton Mifflin, 1966), 384.
15. William E. Leuchtenburg, *Franklin D. Roosevelt and the New Deal, 1932–1940* (New York: Harper and Row, 1963), 157.
16. Ted Case, *Power Plays* (Seattle, WA: Thriftbooks, 2013), 75.
17. "George Norris," United States Senate , accessed September 16, 2021, https://www.senate.gov/artandhistory/history/minute/George_Norris.htm.
18. National Rural Electric Cooperative Association 21st Century Cooperative Committee, *The Electric Cooperative Purpose: A Compass for the 21st Century* (Arlington, VA: NRECA, 2013).

19. Mark Murphy, "The Dunning-Kruger Effect Helps Explain Why People Resist Hearing Constructive Criticism." *Forbes*, January 24, 2017.

20. Malcom Gladwell, *The Bomber Mafia* (New York: Little, Brown and Company, 2021), 32.

Chapter 1: The Electric Cooperative Purpose

1. Richard Pence and Patrick Dahl, *The Next Greatest Thing* (Washington, DC: National Rural Electric Cooperative Association, 1984), 61.

2. Iron Butterfly, *In-A-Gadda-Da-Vida, In-A-Gadda-Da-Vida*, Atlantic Records, 1968, album.

3. "Rural Electrification Act (REA) (1935)," The Living New Deal, accessed September 16, 2021, https://livingnewdeal.org/glossary/rural-electrification-administration-rea-1935/.

4. Ibid.

5. Ibid.

6. Ibid.

7. Frank Gallant, "Flashbacks: Postmarked 'REA,'" *Rural Electric Magazine*, May 4, 2020.

8. Pence and Dahl, *The Next Greatest Thing*, 227.

9. National Rural Utilities Cooperative Finance Corporation, "Our Industry Has Changed A Lot in the Past 45 years: Our Commitment to Our Member-Owners Has Not," 2014, https://portal.nrucfc.coop/content/dam/cfc_assets/public_tier/Public%20Docs/AboutCFC/FINAL%20CFC%20Intro%20brochure%202020 14.pdf.

10. Ibid.

11. NRECA, *The Electric Cooperative Purpose*.

12. Mark J. Perry, "Fortune 500 Firms 1955 v. 2017: Only 60 Remain, Thanks to the Creative Destruction That Fuels Economic Prosperity," AEI, October 20, 2017, https://www.aei.org/carpe-diem/fortune-500-firms-1955-v-2017-only-12-remain-thanks-to-the-creative-destruction-that-fuels-economic-prosperity/.

13. NRECA, *The Electric Cooperative Purpose*, 1–6.

14. Ibid, 17.

15. "State Marijuana Laws in 2019 Map," Governing: The Future of States and Localities, November 7, 2012 (updated June 25, 2019), https://www.governing.com/archive/state-marijuana-laws-map-medical-recreational.html.

16. USDA Rural Development [home page], accessed September 16, 2021, www.rd.usda.gov.

17. NRECA, *The Electric Cooperative Purpose*, 1–6.

18. Ibid, 51.

19. "Willy Wonka and the Chocolate Factory: Movie Quotes," Rotten Tomatoes, accessed September 16, 2021, https://www.rottentomatoes.com/m/willy_wonka_and_the_chocolate_factory/quotes/.

Chapter 2: We're the Helpers

1. "NRECA International: We Power Communities and Empower People to Improve Their Quality Of Life," NRECA International, accessed September 16, 2021, nrecainternational.coop.
2. "Letter of James: Discipleship Lessons on Practical Christianity," JesusWalk, accessed September 16, 2021, http://www.jesuswalk.com/books/james.htm.
3. Matt. 5:16.
4. "Youth Programs [2020]," NRECA: America's Electric Cooperatives, accessed September 16, 2021, www.electric.coop.
5. Minnesota Rural Electric Association [home page], accessed September 16, 2021, www.mrea.org.
6. "God Helps Those Who Help Themselves: Is It in the Bible?" Christianity.com, April 1, 2016.
7. Matt. 7:25–27.
8. "Veterans Take Honor Flight to Washington, D.C., September 28, 2012," Electric Cooperatives of South Carolina, accessed September 16, 2021, https://www.ecsc.org/content/veterans-take-honor-flight-washington-dc.
9. Prov. 18:15 ["The heart of the discerning acquires knowledge"].
10. "Dolly Parton's Imagination Library," Oregon Trail Electric Cooperative, accessed September 16, 2021, https://www.otec.coop/dolly-partons-imagination-library.
11. Margaret Wise Brown and Clement Hurd, *Over the Moon: A Collection of First Books* (New York: HarperCollins, 2006).
12. "Franklin D. Roosevelt > Quotes > Quotable Quote," Goodreads, accessed September 16, 2021, https://www.goodreads.com/quotes/35186-the-test-of-our-progress-is-not-whether-we-add.
12. Geoffrey James, "45 Quotes From Mr. Rogers That We All Need Today," *Inc.*, August 5, 2019.
14. "George Will, ABC TV News Personality and Columnist [audio recording]," Landon Lectures Series on Public Issues, Kansas State University, April 15, 1987, https://www.k-state.edu/landon/speakers/george-will/audio.html.

Chapter 3: RUS: Providing for the Least of Them

1. Matt. 25:40, 2020.
2. John Cromartie, "Rural America at A Glance: 2017 Edition," Economic Information Bulletin 182, U.S. Department of Agriculture, November 2017.
3. Robert Caro, *The Years of Lyndon Johnson: The Path To Power* (New York: Random House), 504.
4. Ibid, 576–77.
5. Ted Case, *Power Plays* (Seattle, WA: Thriftbooks, 2013), 133–43.
6. Ibid, 79–88.
7. USDA Rural Development [home page], accessed September 16, 2021, www.rd.usda.gov.

8. Tina Casey, "2018 Farm Bill Includes Key Renewable Energy Program," Clean Technica, December 27, 2018.
9. USDA Rural Development home page.
10. Ibid.
11. Richard Franklin Bensel, *Passion and Preferences: William Jennings Bryan and the 1896 Democratic National Convention* (Cambridge, UK: Cambridge University Press, 2008).

Chapter 4: 7 Deadly Sins Supersede the 7 Cooperative Principals

1. Christopher Ingraham, "I Called This Place 'America's Worst Place To Live': Then I Went There," *Washington Post*, September 3, 2015.
2. Red Lake Electric Cooperative, *Volts and Jolts*, July/August 2018, https://www.redlakeelectric.com/wp-content/uploads/2018/08/JulyAug-2018-VJ_Web.pdf.
3. Jim Cooper, "Electric Co-Operatives: From New Deal to Bad Deal?" *Harvard Journal on Legislation* 45, no. 2 (2008): 335–75.
4. Avery G. Wilks, "SC Utility's Customers Fired Their Board After Pay Scandal: Now They're Taking Over," *The State*, December, 28, 2016.
5. Mark Ballard and David Mitchell, "Eye-Popping Pay, Perks at Louisiana Electric Co-Ops Sparks Investigation," *Baton Rouge Advocate*, September 19, 2018.
6. Mark Ballard, "Rural Co-ops Sue Over Regulators' Authority to Determine Board Benefits," *The Advocate*, June 25, 2019.
7. "Black Worrior EMC Members File for an Injunction to Stop Vote on Bylaw Changes," *Greene County Democrat*, April 27, 2017.
8. Matt Grimley, "Just How Democratic are Rural Electric Cooperatives," Institute for Self-Reliance, January 13, 2016.
9. National Rural Utilities Cooperative Finance Corporation (CFC), *Education & Training Catalogue: 2019–2020*, https://www.rtfc.coop/content/dam/nrucfc/public-tier/documents/events-and-training/Professional_Develoment_Training_Catalog.pdf.
10. "We Own Our Cooperatives," We Own It, accessed September 16, 2021, www.weown.it.
11. Laura Vanderkam, "Why It's So Hard to Change a Bad First Impression," Fast Company, August, 9, 2016.
12. Jane Meyer, "Covert Operations," *The New Yorker*, August 23, 2010.
13. Nigel Jaquiss, "While Portlanders Vote Nov. 6 on a Risky New Tax to Fund Energy Efficiency, Californians Move Forward with a Smarter Approach," *Willamette Week*, October 31, 2018.
14. NRECA, *The Electric Cooperative Purpose*, 4
15. "Are Minnesota Electric Co-Ops Informing Their Member-Owners About Basic Policies – and How to Have a Voice?" Minnesota Local Energy Project, accessed September 16, 2021, www.mnlocalenergyproject.org.

Chapter 5: Governance Comeuppance

1. Debra Jeter, Randall S. Thomas, and Harwell Wells, "Democracy and Dysfunction: Rural Electric Cooperatives and the Surprisingly Persistence of the Separation of Ownership and Control," *Alabama Law Review* 69 (2018).
2. Ibid, 365.
3. Ibid, 386–88.
4. Ibid, 388.
5. Ibid, 389.
6. Ibid, 397.
7. Tom Henry, "Current $61M Bribery Allegation Opens Old Wounds for FirstEnergy," *Pittsburgh Post-Gazette*, August 2, 2020.
8. FirstEnergy [home page], accessed September 16, 2021, www.firstenergycorp.com.
9. Clayton M. Christensen, *The Innovator's Dilemma: When New Technologies Cause Great Firms to Fail* (Boston, MA: Harvard Business Review Press, 2016).
10. Abha Bhattaral, "Sears Is Suing Steven Mnuchin and Other Former Board Members," *Washington Post*, August 19, 2019.
11. Thomas Gryta and Ted Mann, *Lights Out, Pride, Delusion and the Fall of General Electric* (Boston: Houghton Mifflin Harcourt, 2020).
12. Ibid, 10.
13. Ibid, 299.
14. Ibid, 21.
15. Ibid, 267.
16. Ibid, 315.
17. John Carreyrou, *Bad Blood: Secrets and Lies in a Silicon Valley Startup* (New York: Knopf, 2018).
18. "Examining Co-Op Governance: NRECA-CFC Member Task Force to Look at Governance Practices," NRECA, March 14, 2017, https://www.electric.coop/examining-electric-cooperative-governance-nreca.
19. Vern Dosch, Wally Goulet, and Tracy Finneman, *Wired Differently: How to Spark Better Results with a Cooperative Business Model, Servant Leadership, And Shared Values* (Oakville, Ontario: Milner, 2015).
20. NRUCFC, *Education & Training Catalogue, 2019–2020*.
21. "Examining Co-Op Governance," NRECA.
22 Bill George, *True North: Discover Your Authentic Leadership* (San Francisco, CA: Jossey-Bass, 2007).
23. Kerie Kerstetter, "S&P 500 Trend Report: Board Composition, Diversity and Beyond," Diligent Insights, April 19, 2019.
24. "Examining Co-Op Governance," NRECA.
25. Labor Neighbor Research & Training Center and ACORN International, "Democracy Lost & Discrimination Found: The Crisis in Rural Electric Cooperatives in the South," Research and Advocacy Report, Rural Power Project, May 6, 2016, https://ruralpowerproject.org/wp-content/uploads/2016/02/Rural-Power___Final.pdf.
26. Jeter, Thomas, and Wells, "Democracy and Dysfunction," 390.
27. Labor Neighbor Research and ACORN, "Democracy Lost & Discrimination Found."

28. Personal communication with Anne Mayberry (RUS, Rural Development, USDA), November 3, 2020.

29. Eric Weiner, *The Geography of Genius: A Search for the World's Most Creative Places from Ancient Athens to Silicon Valley* (New York: Simon and Schuster, 2016).

30. "Different is Better: Why Diversity Matters in the Boardroom," Russell Reynolds Associates, accessed September 16, 2021, https://www.russellreynolds.com/insights/thought-leadership/different-is-better-why-diversity-matters-in-the-boardroom.

31. Jeter, Thomas, and Wells, "Democracy and Dysfunction," 388.

32. Ibid.

Chapter 6. What's in a Name?

1. "Speaker of the House Howell Cobb of Georgia, October 9, 1868," History, Art & Archives, U.S. House of Representatives, accessed September 16, 2021, https://history.house.gov/Historical-Highlights/1851-1900/1868_10_09_Howell_Cobb/.

2. Sarah Ferris, "Pelosi Removes Paintings of Confederate Leaders from Capitol," *Politico*, June 18, 2020.

3. "Cobb, Thomas Willis, 1784–1830," History, Art & Archives, U.S. House of Representatives, accessed September 16, 2021, https://history.house.gov/People/Detail/11140.

4. "Audit's Verdict on Cobb EMC's Brown? 'A Bully, Not a Leader,'" *Marietta Daily Journal*, June 20, 2015.

5. Kim Isaza, "EMC Directors Admonished: Judge Scolds Group for Stalling Tactics, Demands to Know Former CEO Brown's Pay Since Settlement," *Marietta Daily Journal*, August 13, 2011.

6. "Cobb EMC Reaches $98 Million Settlement," *Marietta Daily Journal*, October 11, 2013.

7. Bob Nightengale, "Despite Hate Mail, Threats, Hank Aaron 'Was Never Scared,'" *USA Today*, April 8, 2020.

8. Adam Alter, "What's In a Name? Everything," BigThink, May 15, 2013.

Chapter 7: What We Should Have Done on Climate Change

1. Powerplant and Industrial Fuel Use Act, H.R. 5146, 95th Cong. (1977–1998).

2. "Most Coal Plants in the United States Were Built before 1990," U.S. Energy Information Administration, April 17, 2017, https://www.eia.gov/todayinenergy/detail.php?id=30812.

3. Tim McDonnell, "America's Dirtiest Power Companies, Ranked," *Mother Jones*, July 14, 2015.

4. S.Res.98 - A resolution expressing the sense of the Senate regarding the conditions for the United States becoming a signatory to any international agreement on greenhouse gas emissions under the United Nations Framework Convention on Climate Change, 105th Cong. (1997–1998).

5. Jennifer Lee and Andrew C. Revkin, "Senate Defeats Climate Bill, But Proponents see Silver Lining," *New York Times*, October 31, 2003.
6. Kate Sheppard, "Everything You Always Wanted to Know About the Waxman-Markey Energy/Climate Bill—In Bullet Point," Grist, June 4, 2009.
7. Ibid.
8. Christa Marshall, "Rural Electric Co-ops Threaten Climate Deal," *New York Times*, June 19, 2009.
9. Thomas Chen, "What the U.S. Midterm 'Shellacking' Means for Energy Policy," State of the Planet, November 29, 2010.
10. Michael Greenstone, "Americans Appear Willing to Pay for a Carbon Tax Policy," *New York Times*, September 15, 2016.
11. Emily Ekins, "68% of Americans Wouldn't Pay $10 a Month in Higher Electric Bills to Combat Climate Change," Cato Institute, March 8, 2019.
12. Frank Newport, "Americans' Global Warming Concerns Continue to Drop: Multiple Indicators Show Less Concern, More Feelings That Global Warming Is Exaggerated," Gallup, May 11, 2010.
13. Alex Tyson, "How Important Is Climate Change to Voters in the 2020 Election?" Pew Research Center, October 6, 2020.
14. Joe Smyth, "Replacing Coal with Renewables Could Save Energy Customers $8 Billion a Year, Financial Analysts Find," DeSmog, January 14, 2020.
15. Duke University, "Replacing Coal with Gas or Renewables Saves Billions of Gallons of Water," ScienceDaily, 21 October 2019.
16. Silvio Maracci, "Renewable Energy Prices Hit Record Lows: How can Utilities Benefit From Unstoppable Solar and Wind?" *Forbes*, January 21, 2020.
17. Mark Dyson and Alex Engel, *A Low-Cost Energy Future for Western Cooperatives* (Basalt, CO: Rocky Mountain Institute, 2018).
18. Brian Eckhouse, "Solar and Wind Cheapest Sources of Power in Most of the World," *Bloomberg Green*, April 28, 2020.
19. Robert Bryce, "Wind Power Is an Attack on Rural America," *Los Angeles Times*, February 27, 2017.
20. Robert Bryce, "Testimony Before the U.S. Senate Energy Committee and Natural Resources Committee," Manhattan Institute, April 11, 2019, https://www.manhattan-institute.org/testimony/senate-energy-natural-resources-innovation-climate.
21. Vaclav Smil, *Energy Myths and Realities: Bringing Science to the Energy Policy Debate* (Washington, DC: American Enterprise Institute Press, 2010).
22. "AWEA Releases Wind Powers America Annual Report 2019," Electrical Wholesaling, April 27, 2020, https://www.ewweb.com/green-market/article/21129785/awea-releases-wind-powers-america-annual-report-2019.
23. John Farrell, "A $6 Billion Opportunity for the Rural Energy Economy," ILSR, July 25, 2014.
24. "Rural Electrification 2.0 Report and Fact Sheet," We Own It, June 20, 2019.
25. Rural Act of 2019, H.R. 2147, 116th Cong. (2019–2020).
26. Esther Whieldon and Gaurang Dholakia, "Forgiving Co-Ops' Federal Coal Debt to Promote Renewables Faces Hurdles," S&P Global Market Intelligence, October 9, 2019.

Chapter 8: The New Green Deal (Why It Might Not Matter)

1. Sarah Pulliam Bailey, "10 Key Excerpts from Pope Francis's Encyclical on the Environment," *Washington Post*, June 18, 2015.
2. Douglas Holtz-Eakin, "Analyzing the Green New Deal," American Action Forum, March 26, 2019.
3. Danielle Kurzleen, "Rep. Alexandria Ocasio-Cortez Releases Green New Deal Outline," NPR, February 7, 2019.
4. Dino Grandoni and Felecia Sonmez, "Senate Defeats Green New Deal, as Democrats Call Vote a 'Sham,'" *Washington Post*, March 26, 2019.
5. "State Renewable Portfolio Standards and Goals," National Conference of State Legislatures, April 17, 2020, https://www.ncsl.org/research/energy/renewable-portfolio-standards.aspx.
6. Drew Bond, "How Rural States are Leading the Clean Energy Revolution," American Council for Capital Formation, January 21, 2019.
7. "The Regional Greenhouse Gas Initiative: An Initiative of Eastern States of the US," RGGI, accessed September 16, 2021.
8. "Greenhouse Gas Emissions Reduction Targets and Market-Based Policies," National Conference of State Legislatures, January 10, 2020.
9. "Morgan Stanley Commits to Net-Zero Financed Emissions by 2050," Morgan Stanley, September 21, 2020.
10. Catherine Boudreau, "Green Destination, No Road Map," *Politico*, September 29, 2020.
11. Ibid.
12. Joe Smyth, "Basin Electric Faces Growing Pressure on Coal from Co-Ops, Insurers, and Banks," Energy and Policy Institute, November 23, 2020.
13. Dana Nuccitelli, "New Study Finds Incredibly High Carbon Pollution Costs: Especially for the US and India," *Guardian*, October 1, 2018.
14. David Bade, "Minnesota Regulators Finalize Carbon Cost Rules for Utility Procurement," UtilityDive, January 5, 2018.
15. "The EPA Is Rewriting the Most Important Number in Climate Economics," *The Economist*, November, 16, 2017.
16. Umair Irfan, "5 Things to Know About Bernie Sander's Aggressive Climate Strategy," *Vox*, February 19, 2020.
17. Lulia Gheorghiu, "Transitioning US to 100% Renewables by 2030 Will Cost $4.5 Trillion: Wood Mackenzie," UtilityDive, June 28, 2019.
18. Reueters Staff, "U.S. Fracking Boom Added 725,000 Jobs—Study," Reuters, November 6, 2015.
19. Trevor Houser and Hannah Pitt, "Preliminary US Emissions Estimates for 2019," Rhodium Group, January 7, 2020.
20. Steven Mufson, "U.S. Greenhouse Gas Emission Fell Slightly in 2019," *Washington Post*, January 7, 2020.
21. Jessica McDonald, "How Potent is Methane?" FactCheck.org, September 24, 2019.
22. Gavin Bade, "Power to the People: Bernie Calls for Federal Takeover of Electricity Production," *Politico*, February 2, 2020.
23. Matt Viser and Dino Grandoni, "Biden, in New Climate Plan, Embraces More Aggressive Steps," *Washington Post*, July 14, 2020.

24. "Energy Related Carbon Dioxide Emission by State, 2005–2016," U.S. Energy Information Administration, February 27, 2011, https://www.eia.gov/environment/emissions/state/analysis/.

25. "Comparison of Cap-and-Trade Programs: California, Ontario, Quebec and Oregon SB 1070*," Oregon Legislature, n.d., accessed September 16, 2021, https://www.oregonlegislature.gov/helm/workgroup_materials/program%20comparison%20chart%2010%2017%2017.pdf.

26. "Oregon Legislators Look to Address Wildfire Bills in 2021," KGW8 News, September 15, 2020.

27. Connor Radnovich, "Oregon House Republicans Join Senate in Walk Out in Protest of Cap-And-Trade," *Statesman-Journal*, February 25, 2020.

28. McGinley v. Wheat Belt Public Power Dust., 325 N.W. 2nd 915 (1983).

29. Tom Scheck, "Minn. House Adopts '25 Percent by 2025' Green Energy Goal," MPR News, February 20, 2007.

30. Chris Mooney, "Your Home Water Heater May Soon Double as a Battery," *Washington Post*, February 24, 2016.

31. "The Public Utility Regulatory Policies Act of 1978," American Public Power Association Issue Brief, January 2020, https://www.publicpower.org/system/files/documents/PURPA%20-%20January%202020.pdf.

32. Ibid.

33. Danielle Powers, "Has the Public Utilities Regulatory Policy Act ("PURPA"} Outlived its Purpose?" Concentric Energy Advisors, December 12, 2018.

34. John Farrell, "Could Minnesota's 'Value of Solar' Make Everyone a Winner?" Institute for Local Self-Reliance, March 13, 2014.

35. "State Net Metering Policies," National Conference of State Legislatures, November 20, 2017, https://www.ncsl.org/research/energy/net-metering-policy-overview-and-state-legislative-updates.aspx.

36. Herman K. Trabish, "Unnecessary Complexity? Assessing New York and California's Landmark DER Proceedings," UtilityDive, April 4, 2018.

37. Gretchen Baake, *The Grid: The Fraying Wires Between Americans and Our Energy Future* (New York: Bloomsbury, 2016), 69.

38. Ibid, 71.

39. "How to Read Your SolarCity Quote," EnergySage, accessed September 16, 2021, https://news.energysage.com/read-solarcity-ppa-contract-lease-agreement-quote/.

40. Ibid.

41. NRECA, *The Electric Cooperative Purpose.*

Chapter 9: The Cost of Climate

1. Bill McKibben, "Do We Actually Need More Gas Stations?" *The New Yorker*, March 24, 2021.

2. Steven Loveday, "The Cheapest Electric Cars in 2021," *U.S. News and World Report*, August 12, 2020.

3. "Coalition Opposing New Gas Stations," CONGAS, accessed September 16, 2021, http://con-gas.org.

4.   Tam Hunt, "Swanson's Law and Making US Solar Scale like Germany," GreenTech Media, November 24, 2014.

5.   Bjorn Lomborg, *False Alarm: How Climate Change Panic Costs Us Trillions, Hurts the Poor, and Fails to Fix the Planet* (New York: Basic Books, 2020), 123.

6.   Melissa Denchak, "Paris Climate Agreement: Everything you Need to Know," NRDC, February 19, 2021.

7.   Wikipedia, "Kellogg-Briand Pact," last modified August 27, 2021, https://en.wikipedia.org/wiki/Kellogg%E2%80%93Briand_Pact.

8.   Lomborg, *False Alarm*, 121.

9.   Ed Hirs, "Why Texans Are Cold and in the Dark," *Washington Post*, February 18, 2021.

10. Lomborg, *False Alarm*, 108.

11. Ibid, 107.

12. Ibid, 173.

13. Bob Ward, "A Closer Examination of the Fantastical Numbers in Bjorn Lomborg's New Book," London School of Economics and Political Science, August 10, 2020.

14. Lomborg, *False Alarm*, 221.

Chapter 10: Baker v. Carr

1.   Ron Elving, "Cities and Immigrants Drove Census Controversy—100 Years Ago," NPR, July 10, 2019.

2.   U.S. Advisory Commission on Intergovernmental Relations, *Apportionment of State Legislatures* (Washington, DC: U.S. Govt. Printing Office, 1962), 32.

3.   Ibid, 37.

4.   Ibid, 38.

5.   Emily Badger, "As American as Apple Pie? The Rural Votes Disproportionate Slice of Power," *New York Times*, November 20, 2016.

6.   Congressional Research Service, "Membership of the 116th Congress: A Profile," updated December 17, 2020, https://crsreports.congress.gov/product/pdf/R/R45583.

Chapter 11: Ties that Bind: The All-Requirement Contract

1.   Tri-State Generation and Transmission Association, Inc., and United States of America v. Shoshone River Power, Appeal from the U.S. District Court for the District of Wyoming, U.S. Court of Appeals for the Tenth Circuit (D.C. No. C85-488-K), No. 87-2288, (May 5, 1989), 3.

2.   Ibid, 7, 21, 22.

3.   Ibid, 30–32.

4.   Tri-State Generation and Transmission v. Shoshone River Power Corp. (No. 86-1413), 805 F. 2nd 351, U.S. Court of Appeals, (10th Cir., 1986), point 16

5.   "Basin Electric Member Wright-Hennepin Cooperative Celebrates 75 Years," Basin Electric Power Cooperative, April 2, 2012.

6. "Testimony of Paul Sukut, CEO and General Manager, Basin Electric Power Cooperative Before the Senate Committee on Environment and Public Works," U.S. Senate Committee on Environment and Public Works, February 27, 2019, www.epw.senate.gov.

7. "Beverly Hillbillies Theme Lyrics: The Ballad of Jed Clampett by Paul Henning [released November 26, 1962]," Lyrics on Demand, accessed September 16, 2021, https://lyricsondemand.com/tvthemes/beverlyhillbillieslyrics.html.

8. McKenzie Electric Cooperative, Inc. v. Basin Electric Power Cooperative et al., State of North Dakota, NW Judicial District (November 2019), 11.

9. Ibid, 12.

10. Jill Schramm, "McKenzie Electric, Basin Electric at Odds over Rates, Synfuels Plant," *Minot   Daily News*, February 4, 2020.

11. McKenzie Electric Cooperative, Inc. v. Basin Electric Power Cooperative et al., State of North Dakota, NW Judicial District (November 2019), 3.

12. Patrick Michaels, "Global Warming Produced a Greener, More Fruitful Plant," Cato Institute, September 13, 2001.

13. Kirk Johnson, "In Colorado, a Power Struggle with the Power Company," *New York Times*, October 30, 2011.

14. J. R. Rogan, "Kit Carson CEO Reyes Says Tri-State Break Has Two Big Advantages," *Taos News*, June 30, 2016.

15. 151 FERC, 61,238, Delta Montrose Electric Association, Docket No. EL15-43-000, issued June 18, 2015.

16. "DMEA Files with PUC Seeking Just and Reasonable Exit Charge from Tri-State," DMEA, December 20, 2018, https://www.dmea.com/dmea-files-puc-seeking-just-and-reasonable-exit-charge-tri-state.

17. Allen Best, "Colorado PUC Commissioner Grills Tri-State Lawyer," *Mountain Town News*, July 14, 2019.

18. Patrick Armijo, "Federal Agency Says Colorado Public Utility Commission Can Rule on Tiff over Contract Buyout," *Durango Herald*, March 23, 2020.

19. Mark Jaffee, "The Electric Cooperative Serving Delta, Montrose Settles on $136.5 Million Fee to Break Up with Tri-State," *Colorado Sun*, April 13, 2020.

20. Ibid.

21. Ibid.

22. Personal communication with Tim Lindall (CEO of Wheat Belt Public Power District, Sidney, Nebraska), August 2020.

23. Mark Pearson, "Electric Co-Ops Closer to Securing Tri-State Exit Fees," *Durango Herald*, July 20, 2020.

24. Emma Penrod, "Colorado PUC Dismisses Exit Fee Complaints against Tri-State, Says FERC and District Courts Have Jurisdiction," UtilityDive, October 26, 2020.

25. "We're Taking Bold Steps," Tri-State, accessed September 16, 2021, https://tristate.coop/our-responsible-energy-plan.

26. Tim McDonnell, "America's Dirtiest Power Companies, Ranked," *Mother Jones*, July 14, 2015.

27. Joe Smyth, "Lignite Energy Council Shouldn't Be Funded By Utility Ratepayers, Minnesota Attorney General Argues," Energy and Policy Institute, May 19, 2021.

28. Joe Brooks, *You Light Up My Life*, Arista Records, 1977, album.
29. Personal communication with Jeff Nelson (retired CEO of East River Electric Power Cooperative, Madison, South Dakota), October 2020.
30. Robert Walton, "FERC Reversal on Electric Co-Op Exit Fee Jurisdiction Could Have a Broader Rate Implications, Analyst Say," UtlityDive, September 3, 2020.

Chapter 12: G&T Governance Course

1. "National Association of Corporate Directors [2021]," GuideStar, accessed September 16, 2021, https://www.guidestar.org/profile/52-2314113.
2. "Alfred P. Sloan Quotes," AZ Quotes, accessed September 16, 2021, https://www.azquotes.com/author/13714-Alfred_P_Sloan.

Chapter 13: Can We Do It Again?

1. Steely Dan, "Do It Again," by Walter Becker and Daniel Fagen, on *Can't Buy a Thrill*, ABC Records, November, 1972.
2. NRECA, *The Electric Cooperative Purpose*, 16.
3. Ibid, 18.
4. "Electric Co-Op Facts and Figures," NRECA, June 23, 2020.
5. Indigo [home page], accessed September 16, 2021, www.indigoag.com.
6. "About Us," Dakota Gasification Company, accessed September 16, 2021, www.dakotagas.com.
7. Lori Kolodny, "The Biggest Breakthrough in Agriculture to Help Feed the Planet May Come from Outer Space," CNBC Disrupter/50, May 15, 2019.
8. Louisa Burwood-Taylor, "Indigo Launches Carbon Market to Incentivize Farmers to Transition to Regenerative Agriculture," AFN, June 12, 2019.
9. Lori Kolodny, "This Is a $15 Trillion Opportunity for Farmers to Flight Climate Change," CNBC Disrupter/50, June 12, 2019.
10. Ibid.
11. Kurt Thelen, "Corn Fields Help Clean Up and Protect the Environment," Michigan State University Extension, June 7, 2007.
12. "The Regional Greenhouse Gas Initiative: An Initiative of Eastern States of the US," RGGI, accessed September 16, 2021, https://www.rggi.org/.
13. "Policy Hub: California Cap and Trade," Center for Climate and Energy Solutions, accessed September 16, 2021, https://www.c2es.org/content/california-cap-and-trade/.
14. "USA-California Cap-and-Trade Program," International Carbon Action Partnership, last update September 15, 2020.
15. Mark Shapiro, "Conning the Climate: Inside the Carbon-Trading Shell Game," *Harper's*, February 2010.
16. "1603 Program: Payments for Specified Energy Property in lieu of Tax Credits," U.S. Department of the Treasury, accessed September 16, 2021, www.home.treasury.gov.
17. Michael J. Boyle, "American Recovery and Reinvestment Act," Investopedia, September 26, 2020.

18. Personal communication with Jeff Nelson (retired CEO of East River Energy Power Cooperative, Madison, South Dakota), September 2020.
19. American Wind Energy Association, "South Dakota Wind Partners: More Than 600 Residents Invest in Seven 1.5 MW Turbines," n.d., http://d3n8a8pro7vhmx .cloudfront.net/windustry/legacy_url/2829/RevisedSouthDakotaWindPartners .pdf?1421784692.
20. Ibid.

Chapter 14: Contemplating the Carbon Individual Retirement Act

1. Climate Action 100+ [home page], accessed September 15, 2020, www.climate action100.org.
2. Jonathan Watts, "We Have 12 Years to Limit Climate Change Catastrophe, Warns UN," *Guardian*, October 7, 2018.
3. "Congressional Testimony of Dr. James Hansen, June 23, 1988," SeaLevel.info, https://www.sealevel.info/1988_Hansen_Senate_Testimony.html.
4. Alex Fox, "Earth Loses 1.2 trillion Tons of Ice Per Year, a Nearly 60% Increase from 1994," *Smithsonian*, January 29, 2021.
5. "State Renewable Portfolio Standards and Goals," National Conference of State Legislatures, April 17, 2020.
6. Alison Cherryholmes (production manager, *RE Magazine*) email correspondence, April 9, 2019: "In 2017, electric distribution co-ops retired over $1.1 billion in capital credits to their member-owners. Rural electric co-ops have returned over $16 billion of equity to their members over the years."
7. Nigel Jaquiss, "While Portlanders Vote Nov. 6 on a Risky New Tax to Fund Energy Efficiency, Californians Move Forward with a Smarter Approach," *Willamette Week*, October 31, 2018.
8. Richard Thaler and Cass Sunstein, *Nudge: Improving Decisions about Health, Wealth, and Happiness* (New Haven, CT: Yale University Press, 2008).
9. John Sullivan, "Happy Birthday! The IRA Turns 45," 401kSpecialist, September 13, 2019.

Chapter 15: The Cap Rock Way

1. Reference for Business Encyclopedia, "History of Cap Rock Energy Corp.," accessed September 16, 2021, https://www.referenceforbusiness.com/history2/25/Cap-Rock -Energy-Corporation.html.
2. Ibid.
3. Personal communication with Steve Collier, October 22, 2020.
4. Reference for Business Encyclopedia, "History of Cap Rock Energy Corp."
5. Richard Rudolph and Scott Ridley, *Power Struggle: The Hundred-Year War over Electricity* (New York: Harper and Row, 1986), 76.
6. Wikipedia, "Public Utility Holding Company Act of 1935," last modified August 27, 2021, https://en.wikipedia.org/wiki/Public_Utility_Holding_Company_Act_of_1935.

7. Reference for Business Encyclopedia, "History of Cap Rock Energy Corp."
8. Robert Elder Jr., "Co-ops Prepare for World of Electricity Competition," *Wall Street Journal*, April 16, 2003.
9. Ibid.
10. Kurt Johnson, "Editor's Corner," Johnson Consulting, http://www.gismedia.com/texelect/medcoa16.htm.
11. "Lobby Watch: Revolving-Door Lobbyist Adopts So-Craddick Method," Texans for Public Justice, November 21, 2002.
12. Texas Coalition for Affordable Power, *Deregulated Electricity in Texas: A History of Retail Competition* (Addison, TX: Author, 2014).
13. Editor, "Cap Rock Electric Co-Op Announces Release of Stocks," *Brady Standard-Herald*, March 1, 2002.
14. Ibid.
15. "Cap Rock Energy Corporation to Be Acquired by Lindsay Goldberg [press release]," Cap Rock Energy, November 7, 2005, https://www.lindsaygoldbergllc.com/wp-content/uploads/2019/04/11072005.pdf.
16. Ibid.
17. "Sharyland Signs Deal to Buy Cap Rock for $221.5 Million," *Dallas Morning News*, December 17, 2009.
18. Wikipedia, "H. L. Hunt," last modified September 15, 2021, https://en.wikipedia.org/wiki/H._L._Hunt.
19. Sempra Energy, *2018 Annual Report: Building North America's Premier Energy Infrastructure Company* (San Diego, CA: Author), https://www.sempra.com/sites/default/files/microsites/2018_annualreport/.
20. Loren Steffy, "Electric Mayhem," *Texas Monthly*, August 2016.
21. Ibid.
22. "Questions Rise at West Texas Utility: Midland's Cap Rock," *MRT*, March 20, 2005.
23. Securities and Exchange Commission, "Commission File 0-32667: Cap Rock Energy Corporation," December 31, 2001, https://sec.report/Document/0000912057-02-013399/.

Chapter 16: 1st Rochdale

1. Edward Yaker, Fredric S. Goldner, and Thomas Thompson, "The Cooperative Alternative Case Study: The First Urban Electric Cooperative," n.d., https://www.aceee.org/files/proceedings/2000/data/papers/SS00_Panel5_Paper32.pdf.
2. Shannon Terrell-Ernest, "Let There Be Light (and Heat, and Telecommunications): A Closer Look at the 1st Rochdale Cooperative," Cooperator News New York, October 2001.
3. David Thompson, "Cooperative Principles Then and Now," *Co-Operative Grocer* #53 (July–August 1994, archived from the original of October 10, 2007).
4. Wikipedia, "Cooperative Hall of Fame," last modified August 21, 2021, https://en.wikipedia.org/wiki/Cooperative_Hall_of_Fame.
5. Terrell-Ernest, "Let There Be Light."
6. "Aggregation Initiatives in the U.S.: Gregory Wortham, Senior Corporate

Counsel, National Rural Electric Cooperative Association before the Consumer, Environment and Education Task Force of the Subcommittee Studying Electric Utility Restructuring, The General Assembly, Commonwealth of Virginia, September 17, 1998," Commonwealth of Virginia, Division of Legislative Services, http://dls .virginia.gov/groups/sjr91/91798/917NRECA.HTM.

7. Terrell-Ernest, "Let There Be Light."
8. Diane Henry, "How to Cut Utility Cost in a Co-op," *New York Times*, November 28, 1982.
9. Raanan Geberer, "Submetering Your Building's Electricity," Cooperator News New York, September 2011.
10 Glenn English (retired NRECA CEO) email correspondence, September 1, 2020.
11. Ibid.
12. Geberer, "Submetering Your Building's Electricity."
13. Terrell-Ernest, "Let There Be Light."
14. "New York to Use Renewable Energy to Alleviate Power Grid," Renewable Energy World, December 18, 2000.
14. Ibid.
15. Martin Lowery (retired NRECA VP) email correspondence, August 9, 2020.
16. Personal communication with Ed Yakey (1st Rochdale Incorporator), August 30, 2020.

Chapter 17: Co-op Evangelism

1. "Idaho Power, CP National Cancel Sale," UPI, December 31, 1986.
2. "OTEC Roots: A One-Cent Membership Fee and CFC," *CFC Solutions News Bulletin*, February 4, 2013.
3. Jayson Jacoby, "Peggi Timm Dies," *Baker City Herald*, July 26, 2013.
4. "10 Best Ruth Bader Ginsburg Quotes Through the Years," CNN, September 19, 2020.
5. Wikipedia, "Enrico Fermi Nuclear Generating Station," last modified June 30, 2021, https://en.wikipedia.org/wiki/Enrico_Fermi_Nuclear_Generating_Station.
6. Personal communications with Bill Collet, September 25, 2020.
7. Kaua'i Island Utility Cooperative, "More Than Half Full: KIUC 2019 Annual Report," https://website.kiuc.coop/sites/kiuc/files/documents/annualreport /AnnualReport19_web.pdf.
8. Personal communications with Bill Collet, September 25, 2020.
9. James Bridges, dir., Michael Douglas, prod., *The China Syndrome*, Columbia Pictures, 1979.
10. Jackson Browne, Graham Nash, John Hall, and Bonnie Raitt, prod., *No Nukes: The Muse Concerts for a Non-Nuclear Future*, Asylum Records, November 1979, album.
11. "Atomic Energy Commission," U.S. NRC, updated March 9, 2021, https://www .nrc.gov/reading-rm/basic-ref/glossary/atomic-energy-commission.html.
12. ANS Nuclear Cafe, "Eisenhower's Atomic Power for Peace III: CAP and Power Demonstration Reactors," NuclearNewswire, March 20, 2014.
13. Wikipedia, "Clinch River Breeder Reactor," last modified January 29, 2021, https:// en.wikipedia.org/wiki/Clinch_River_Breeder_Reactor_Project.

14. Peter Thomson, "LACBWR Storage," *LaCrosse Tribune*, October 8, 2015.
15. David Wilma, "Washington Public Power Supply System (WPPSS)," HistoryLink.org, July 10, 2003.
16. Ibid.
17. "Seabrook Nuclear Power Plant's 12-Year History," UPI, June 23, 1984.
18. Matthew Wald, "Rural Vermont Bearing Brunt of Nuclear Failures," *New York Times*, August 24, 1986.

Chapter 18: Musing Mergers

1. "Electric Power Annual [with date for 2019]," U.S. Energy Information Administration, October 21, 2020, https://www.eia.gov/electricity/annual/.
2. Ibid.
3. Jim Cooper, "Electric Co-Operatives: From New Deal to Bad Deal?" *Harvard Journal on Legislation* 45, no. 2 (2008): 335–75.
4. NRECA: America's Electric Cooperatives [home page], accessed September 16, 2021, www.electric.coop.
5. Rio Grande Electric Co-Op [home page], accessed September 16, 2021, www .riogrande.coop.
6. Cooper, "Electric Co-Operatives." P 163
7. "The Telecommunications Act of 1996," Mitel, accessed September 16, 2021, https:// www.mitel.com/articles/telecommunications-act-1996.
8. NTCA: The Rural Broadband Association [home page], www.ntca.org.
9. Kendra Chamberlain, "Missouri's Battleground for Community Broadband," *Salem News*, October 15, 2019.
10. Hilda Legg, "Partnership for Rural Broadband," *BroadbandCommunities Magazine*, January/February 2017.
11. Ibid.

Chapter 19: Call Sheldon

1. Kevin Kruse, "Stephen Covey: 10 Quotes That Can Change Your Life," *Forbes*, July 16, 2012.
2. Steven Johnson, "Examining Co-Op Governance: NRECA-CFC Member Task Force to Look at Governance Practices," NRECA, March 14, 2017, https://www.electric .coop/examining-electric-cooperative-governance-nreca.

Chapter 20: Ask the Chairman

1. "Sen. Craig Thomas," GovTrack, accessed September 16, 2021, https://www.govtrack .us/congress/members/craig_thomas/300097.
2. "Sen. Saxby Chambliss," accessed September 16, 2021, https://www.govtrack.us /congress/members/saxby_chambliss/300021

3. "Sen. Dave Durenberger," accessed September 16, 2021, https://www.govtrack.us/congress/members/david_durenberger/403669

4. "Harold P. LeVander Biography," Minnesota Historical Society, accessed September 16, 2021, https://mnhs.gitlab.io/archive/governors-of-minnesota-collections/collections.mnhs.org/governors/index.php/10004227.html.

5. "Commemorating the Staggers Act," Association of American Railroads, accessed September 16, 2021, https://www.aar.org/campaigns/the-staggers-rail-act-40th-anniversary/.

6. Richard Rudolph and Scott Ridley, *Power Struggle: The Hundred-Year War over Electricity* (New York: Harper & Row, 1986).

7. Frontline, "Regulation: What Is FERC?" PBS, accessed September 16, 2021, https://www.pbs.org/wgbh/pages/frontline/shows/blackout/regulation/ferc.htm.

8. "FERC Proposes Policy Statement on State-Determined Carbon Pricing in Wholesale Markets [press release]," FERC, October 15, 2020, https://www.ferc.gov/news-events/news/ferc-proposes-policy-statement-state-determined-carbon-pricing-wholesale-markets.

9. Josh Siegel, "Neil Chatterjee Replaced as FERC Chairman after Promoting Carbon Pricing," *Washington Examiner*, November 5, 2020.

10. "Tailpipe Emission Standards," American Council for Energy-Efficient Economy, accessed September 16, 2021, https://database.aceee.org/state/tailpipe-emission-standards.

11. Sean Baur, "Going Beyond Order 841 to More Meaningful FERC Storage Policy," UtilityDive, September 1, 2020.

12. Paul Clampoli, "Groups Say Storage Orders Ignore Federal/State Jurisdiction Bright Line," American Public Power Association, November 12, 2020.

13. Craig Cano, "FERC Order No. 2222: A New Day for Distributed Energy Resources," U.S. FERC Fact Sheet, September 17, 2020.

14. Personal communication with Neil Chatterjee (commissioner, Federal Energy Regulatory Commission), November 11, 2020.

Chapter 21: Abiding Biden

1. Matt. 25 NIV [The Parable of the Ten Virgins].

2. "Fact Sheet: Overview of the Clean Power Plan: Cutting Carbon Pollution from Power Plants," U.S. EPA, May 9, 2017, https://archive.epa.gov/epa/cleanpowerplan/fact-sheet-overview-clean-power-plan.html.

3. Joceylan Durkay, "States' Reactions to EPA Greenhouse Gas Emission Standards," National Conference of State Legislatures, December 28, 2017.

4. Courtney Scobie, "Supreme Court Stays EPA Clean Power Plan," American Bar Association, February 17, 2016.

5. Juliet Ellpern and Annie Linsky, "How Biden Aims to Amp Up the Government's Fight against Climate Change," *Washington Post*, November 11, 2020.

6. "Climate 21 Project," accessed September 16, 2021, www.climate21.org.

7. James Choi, "One of the Most Vivid Arithmetic Failings Displayed by Americans," Economist View, July 23, 2014.

8.   John Denver, vocalist, "Take Me Home, Country Roads," by Bill Danoff, Taffy Nivert, and John Denver, on *Poems, Prayers & Promises*, produced by Susan Ruskin and Milton Okun, RCA Records, 1971.

9.   "Colorado Governor Joins Tri-State to Announce Greenhouse Gas Reduction Goals," CoopLawBlog.com, November 16, 2020, https://www.cooplawblog.com/2020/11/colorado-governor-joins-tri-state-to-announce-greenhouse-gas-reduction-goals/.

10. "Electric Co-Op Facts and Figures," NRECA, July 19, 2021.

11. "USDA Halts Loan Program for Rural Coal-Fired Plants," *Mail Tribune*, March 14, 2008.

12. Reuters Staff, "In First for Fed, U.S. Central Bank Says Climate Poses Stability Risks," Reuters, November 9, 2020.

13. John Rotoni, "What is ESG Investing," The Motley Fool, October 5, 2020.

14. "Climate Action 100+," Climate Initiative Platform, accessed September 16, 2021, https://climateinitiativesplatform.org/index.php/Climate_Action_100%2B.

Chapter 22: The Jetsons

1.   "The Jetsons [TV Series, 1962–1963]," IMDb, accessed September 16, 2021, https://www.imdb.com/title/tt0055683/.

2.   "Community Power, Not Corporate Power," Institute For Local Self-Reliance, accessed September 16, 2021, www.ilsr.org.

3.   Lilli Ambort and John Farrel, "Report: Could Existing Water Pipes Replace Dirty Energy Utilities?" Institute for Local Self-Reliance, October 13, 2020.

4.   Ibid.

5.   "How Much Does an Air Source Heat Pump Cost?" EnergySage, last updated December 23, 2020, https://www.energysage.com/clean-heating-cooling/air-source-heat-pumps/costs-and-benefits-air-source-heat-pumps/.

6.   Ibid.

7.   Ambort and Farrel, "Report: Could Existing Water Pipes Replace."

8.   Ibid.

Chapter 23: Aspirations Electrification

1.   Alexis Okeowo, "The Heavy Toll of the Black Belt's Wastewater Crisis," *The New Yorker*, November 23, 2020.

2.   Ibid.

3.   Personal communication with Ryan Baker (Washoughal, Washington Utility Department).

4.   Will Whaley, "Uniontown Receives $23M USDA Grant," *Selma Times-Journal*, November 16, 2018.

5.   Personal communication with Gary Harrison (Dixie Electric CEO), October 21, 2020.

6.   Ibid.

7.   Bill Chappell, 'Time' Names its Kid of the Year: Water-Testing Scientist Gitanjali Rao, Time Magazine, December 3, 2020.

CPSIA information can be obtained
at www.ICGtesting.com
Printed in the USA
LVHW031916261121
704483LV00001B/34